Keep Calm & Carry On Learning

A compilation of short stories to help you in your (sales) career

JAMES MCGUINNESS

I dedicate this book to my wife, Jamie, who has put up with me typing late at night and interrupting conversations so I can quickly share a new idea I have with her. To my mum, Glynis, who has always been my moral compass and supported me throughout and, finally, to my wonderful children, Addy and Stevie. If writing makes me happy, they make me feel on cloud nine.

Thank you for taking the time to read this book.

Table of Contents

Introduction	1
The Paintbrush	6
The Wedding Planner	21
The Lemonade Stand	34
The Car Dealership	47
The Vacation	58
The Baker	69
The Detective	80
The Old Coach	93
The Babysitters	106

Introduction

I firmly believe in the old saying, "Everything happens for a reason" – you just might not know what those reasons are at the time. This book is a case in point. It brings together two enduring journeys that have dominated my adult life.

The first is my career.

In 1991, my family lost our home as we went through tough times. I always wanted to be in the corporate world and make a lot of money so that when I had a family of my own they wouldn't go through what mine had experienced. I was also never afraid of hard work, even as a teenager. I didn't know it at the time but my sales career started when I was about 13. My grandad had fought in the Second World War and was determined to sell poppies every November so that veterans got the care and support they needed and so that people did not forget about the war. I would get up at the crack of dawn and sit outside a supermarket with him come rain or shine every Saturday and Sunday. He was determined to both run out of poppies and fill the donation jar every week. This taught me so many fundamental sales skills, most of which are highlighted in this book.

By the time I was 16, I had three jobs. I did my paper round, sold eggs for a local farmer to people in my neighbourhood, and worked all summer in the mailroom of an insurance company run by one of my dad's former employees. Along with others in my class, I also won our district's Young Enterprise Award that year for creating a business that built custom mirrors – one is still on my mum's bathroom wall today!

When my friend died at 18, I decided to move away from my home town and found myself going to university four hours away. They had a course on financial services, something that could offer career opportunities in that corporate world I craved. I studied every possible division of business – Marketing, Product, HR, Operations, Customer Support – in fact, everything except sales!

After I graduated, I applied to work in about 30+ banks and insurance companies in London and was rejected by all, so I decided to widen my search. In September 2004, I applied to be a salesperson at a cyber security startup company. I had no sales experience, didn't know what cyber security was, but I was given a shot and that changed my career. I was one of the first 10 employees there and we worked our socks off, sometimes until 2am. I didn't get any real training, so when the company grew, I was tasked with training others, and that started my path towards leadership and coaching.

Fast forward to today (2024) and for the last 20 years, I have been in technology sales and leadership. Most of my career has also been in startups. I have hired and trained hundreds of sales professionals and sold solutions into multiple countries around the world. I've never claimed to be the best salesperson, leader or coach but, after being in this arena for such a long time and surrounding myself with some fantastic salespeople, leaders and executives, I've seen a lot and have a wealth of experience to share.

The second journey is my love of writing.

For as long as I can remember, I have been creative, thinking up numerous different stories. When I was around 14, I wrote a book about cowboys. I clearly remember writing it and even acting it out in my bedroom. I was so embarrassed to be a writer that I never told anyone about it. I was already being bullied and this would have added fuel to the fire.

When I was in my twenties, I wrote another book called, *Moment of Truth*. Again, I only told a few people and it got lost on an old laptop somewhere. When I moved to America, I finally became comfortable expressing who I was and I started getting more ideas for books to write. I started to write *Stars Will Guide You Home*, based loosely on my grandparents' experiences during the Second World War and, in 2019, I self published it.

Fast forward to today, and my favourite hobby is writing. As well as this book, I'm in the process of writing numerous other stories. I know my books are not perfect – I self publish so I'm aware there may be mistakes in them – and they may not be everyone's cup of tea but, I'm proud of who I am and what I publish. I encourage anyone who reads this book to find things that make you happy in life and not be ashamed of them. Believe in yourself! I wish I had learnt this earlier in life.

So, how are these two journeys connected? Well, I started to write these short stories purely to ensure that the training and methodologies I have created over the years were put down in writing. However, as I began writing, I started to incorporate the many lessons learned over the years: lessons from those much smarter than me; lessons from failings; and lessons from practice and doing things over and over again.

My goal for this book is that it will help everyone in some way, even if that is a small way. In my opinion, you don't have to be in sales (although given my background, many of the lessons taught will align with this profession) to benefit from the book. My hope is that any person in any role, from doctors to caretakers, accountants to pilots or retail employees, can benefit from reading this book and take at least one lesson away from it. I am, of course, slightly biased! I also hope that this book will help people at all stages of their careers, whether they're just starting out and need advice, are on career breaks or even those in the middle or towards the end of their careers who might be reminded of a best practice or two.

While all of the stories and characters are fictional, they are based on truth and things I have experienced in my life and career. All of the methodologies are those I have created and still use and teach today.

The Paintbrush

Ian had graduated from university in the summer, he had a degree in business and had been top of his class. His big ambition was to work in a tech startup, like others who had graduated before him, but in four months he'd had no success finding a job. Out of the 100 plus applications he'd completed he had only heard back from eight companies and secured just three interviews.

He was broke and his rent was due. He didn't want to move back to live with his mum as she lived an hour away and he had friends where he was. He had also signed an agreement to rent his shared property with four others and didn't want to let them down. So, as he arrived for Thanksgiving at his mum's house he felt a sense of dread that he would have to explain to his family that he was out of work. He would probably have to build up the courage to ask his mum to loan him some money, too, and he knew she didn't have much herself.

When they sat down for dinner he was sat next to his grandad, Steve, who always made him smile. They would talk about sports or play sports, and he had a great love of old music. As soon as they sat down his grandad leaned over to him and said quietly, "Still no work?" Ian put his head down and didn't know how to answer. His grandad could see that this was a painful subject, so he intervened. "I was taught by my grandad to take your time and find a job that ticks all of the following:

1. You have to be passionate about the company. Can you wear their t-shirt with pride and tell your old grandad about it
2. You have to be passionate about the job. You are going to work for probably 40 years, eight hours a day. I've seen far too many people grumble that they hate their job, it's not worth it.
3. You have to be passionate about your boss. Is this person going to teach you new things, help get the best out of you? Don't work for a jerk."

Ian actually found himself nodding with his grandad, it did make sense. However he was broke and needed a job, a good job with a cool office where he could have fun. "Good advice grandad, I can really see myself enjoying working for a tech startup, I'm sure I'll get a role there soon." Grandad Steve continued, "Well, why don't you come work for me for a couple of weeks, until you find this tech startup? I'll pay you $1,500 for two weeks' work".

"Thanks grandad, I appreciate the offer but I really want to work for a tech startup," Ian politely responded. His grandad was a painter and decorator and had been all his life. He was very blue collar and although Ian loved him it was not what he wanted to do. "Okay, if you change your mind let me know." Steve finished the conversation and they started to talk about sport.

That night Ian kept thinking about his grandad's offer. His grandad had not even gone to college, Ian had painted his room before, how hard could it be for a couple of weeks? Plus, the $1,500 would cover his rent and pay his credit card, and his grandad's office was just down the road from him. On Friday morning, he phoned his grandad and asked if the offer still stood. "Of course," replied Steve, "get to my office at 6.30am on Monday."

Monday arrived, Ian got up early and walked 30 minutes to his grandad's office. It was a tiny space in an industrial park but the cold fresh air on the walk woke him up. There was a small sign outside the office and inside there were three desks as well as an area in the back with lots of paint and equipment. Steve met him and was clearly excited to have Ian there.

Ian was introduced to the other two people in his crew. Sofia was a young looking Latino, with eyes that told the story of someone who had seen a lot. She couldn't speak English very well so shook his hand and nodded. Lee was a tall, muscular black guy and, by Ian's guess, was about 40. Ian had actually met him once before and was a little scared of him as he knew that Lee had served prison time years ago.

"Here we go," Ian thought. This was how far he had fallen since the days of guest CEO lecturers and some really bright people around him. Now he was working with a former criminal, an immigrant and someone without a college degree. "What a waste of $80k in college fees," he thought. Ian felt like he was on a conveyor belt as they operated so quickly, loading the van, grabbing coffees from the nearby drive through and then they were on their way.

When they got to the client's house, they unpacked the van and headed into the living room. They started moving the furniture out of the room, then put protective sheets over anything that remained. After that, Lee and Steve picked up paint tins and brushes and Ian naturally did as well. "What are you doing?" Steve asked with a friendly but firm voice. "I thought we were painting today," Ian responded. "We are, you're not. You're not ready or trained to do that. You are on tape and trash duty." Steve took the paintbrush and handed him green paint tape. "You need to make sure that all the borders are taped so no paint can leak through."

Ian was shocked that his grandad had spoken to him in that way and that he would be doing such basic work. He was overqualified for this role, he had experience painting and yet he was the bottom of the pole. However, he took the tape and started protecting the borders, angrily tearing off pieces and sticking them down. After an hour or so, Steve walked over to where Ian had been taping, took a brush and did a long stroke over the tape. "That's just leaked through. Please take up all the tape and do it again carefully." Ian was fuming. He'd already decided that he would not be coming back and that his relationship with his grandad was over.

The day ended and Ian had taped and cleaned out garbage all day. He felt drained and was glad to go home. This had been a huge mistake, he thought. His day, however, was not over. To his surprise, when they got back to the office, he had to clean all the brushes and trays and leave them to dry before they eventually all went home.

The next morning, Ian had set his alarm to get up early. He hadn't slept well with the previous day swirling around his mind. As he awoke he made a decision; he was not a quitter, he never had been and so he forced himself to get up and went to his grandad's office. His grandad simply smiled and said, "Welcome back." They loaded the van and set off. That day's work was at the same place. Ian knew what to expect now and took the tape. Today, however, before he started he asked Sofia if she could show him what to do. As her English was rudimental, she got up and showed him the technique. Ian observed as she pushed her fingers down on the edge and he instantly knew he could be more efficient than the day before. He actually felt good at the end of the day.

The next day was much the same. It was the last day of the project and Ian was impressed how much brighter the rooms they had painted looked. At the end of the day when they were back at the office, the phone rang. Steve answered and Ian could hear some of the call. Steve spoke calmly but assertively, "I understand what you are saying," he started "but what you are asking for is unreasonable. If you want all of that done then the cost will be higher." There was a pause. "I understand, thank you." He turned to the room: "Tomorrow is an office day, be here, same time."

Thursday arrived and Ian found himself at the office all day. The client had cancelled on them and from what Lee had said and from what he deciphered from the call, the client didn't want to pay the agreed amount and wanted more work done than he had originally planned. Ian had no idea what he was going to do all day. He'd downloaded some games on his phone hoping it would be an easy day.

Ian was surprised when Lee and Sofia sat down at their desks and started working. Curiosity got the better of him so he sat down with Sofia to see what she was doing. He was amazed to see her on Excel. He had studied basic accounting but this was way beyond him. She was effortlessly running financial models for the business. Steve popped over and told Ian that before she was forced to abandon her home country because of war, she was the equivalent of a qualified accountant.

That afternoon he sat down with Lee who had been busy working all day. He discovered that Lee was a whizz when it came to web design and marketing, and was currently rebuilding the company's social media sites. Lee and Ian had a good chat. "You know when I was your age I was put in jail," Lee piped up. Ian had wanted to know what had happened to Lee but was afraid to ask. "I needed money, got in with the wrong crowd and one kid stole a car. I was the passenger and therefore part of it. I tried to stop him and even went to the police afterwards to tell them what had happened. I was scared of this kid, he owned a gun but I had to do what's right. The police looked at me as a criminal as well and said I was an accomplice. I got sentenced to 10 years." As he finished, tears streamed down his face.

Ian had hung out with the wrong crowd in the past – that could have been him. He suddenly felt very privileged and lucky. Lee continued, "I was determined not to let my life go to waste. I'd graduated with a degree in marketing before the incident and I was determined that jail wouldn't define me. I continued studying there, and now on days like this I get to put it to use." Ian was shell shocked that Lee also had a degree and felt great remorse for how he had judged him.

Ian was actually able to use his experiences from studying marketing to use, too, and by the end of the day, they'd built an impressive social media presence. All day, Steve had been at the back cleaning brushes and tools.

Friday came about and Ian was glad it was the weekend. They had a client engagement but it was a small apartment. Ian had improved with the taping and completed it quickly. He took the initiative to clean behind the others as they went so that they could all finish early. At the end of the day, Ian just wanted to go home, watch TV and play on his computer games. He was exhausted. But Steve told him that it was tradition that every Friday they went to a local bar and he had to go, too.

Steve bought everyone a drink and they all sat there talking Spanish so that Sofia could be part of the conversation. Steve was fluent, Lee was fairly good but Ian was rusty. Lee translated everything to ensure he was also part of the conversation. Steve was so appreciative of everyone's work that week including Ian's and told them that. But Steve also listened a lot.

During the conversation Ian came to understand that Sofia's four-year-old son was going to play soccer that weekend, that Lee and his girlfriend were going for a hike somewhere and it was also nice for Ian to talk about his plans to attend a music festival. He felt part of a team, something he had always loved. Ian fell fast asleep that Friday after a cocktail of exhaustion and alcohol.

As Monday rolled in Ian almost found himself excited to head back to work for the second week, especially as he was going to get paid that week and he had clearly earned it. That day the work seemed to go effortlessly until Lee accidentally knocked over a can of paint which spilled onto the wooden floors in the lounge. They cleaned it up together and it looked as good as new, but Ian happened to be with his grandad as he was settling the bill and his grandad did something that surprised him. Steve told the client, "I wanted to let you know that I knocked a can over today. We cleaned it, but I have also given you a 20% discount in case the clean-up was not to your standard," He would never have noticed Ian thought and his grandad was throwing money away. His grandad could read his mind and when they stepped away from the customer Steve simply said, "Honesty is the best policy." Ian was really impressed with his grandad for taking ownership.

On Tuesday, Ian woke up early and checked out the social media sites he and Lee had created last week. He was pleasantly surprised to see there were ten reviews and nine of them were positive. However, there was one that was really negative. It said: "These people are overpriced, they promised one thing and delivered on another." Ian was angry; he knew his grandad and the others and that this was not true. As he got to work, he spoke to his grandad who simply shrugged it off. "You can't please everyone and I would rather people be honest than have fake reviews like some of my competitors. My work over the years speaks for itself with the quality we delivered." Ian stayed angry about it for the rest of the day.

The following day, they had a large project that was going to take them until the end of the week. The house was bigger than any house Ian had ever been in and they needed to do the whole downstairs. For the first time he saw his grandad pause and develop a plan. He walked through the three rooms that were being painted, retook measurements then he spoke to everyone on what they needed to do. Ian was still on tape duty but he and Lee were going to take one room, his grandad and Sofia another, and as soon as Ian was done with the first room, he was to tape up the third. At the end of the day, they realised they were behind schedule so they all just carried on working until 8pm.

When they arrived the next day, Ian was starstruck. Peter Barnes was standing there as they arrived. Peter was the CEO of a major technology startup company; he had built the business from scratch and was now on numerous TV shows. This was his house. Lee also recognised him and laughed at Ian and said, "One thing jail taught me was that everyone is flesh and bones, we are all the same in the end."

Friday came around and it was Ian's last day. He was looking forward to his pay, but he'd actually found himself enjoying the last couple of weeks and was almost sad that it was ending. At the office, his grandad called him over and told him to close his eyes. With his first hand he gave Ian a cheque for $1,500, and with his other, a paintbrush. "You earnt this if you want to come back," he said. They all went to the bar again that night after work. Ian found himself loving the conversation even if Lee was mocking him for the way Ian had acted around Peter Barnes. "Please, you were like a giddy teenager following a boyband!" Steve translated and they all laughed at Ian.

Monday came round and Ian found himself in a suit and tie. He was being interviewed for a sales role at a top SaaS company in the city. He sat down opposite the interviewer who looked at him and then at his resume. "I'm not sure how you got an interview here, when your only experience is two weeks at these painters. I want you to justify why you deserve a job," he said. He used a condescending tone and the guy was clearly a top school graduate, who was looking down on Ian.

Ian was calm. "Let me first tell you why my experience is more than suitable for this role, then I will answer how I got an interview here. I may only have two weeks' experience but let me tell you what those two weeks taught me. You see, on day one I was given the taping role, which is a role I felt beneath me but I learnt that everyone has to master the basics first and do jobs they may not want to.

"On day two, I remembered that I am not a quitter. I was ready to quit after the way I'd been treated on my first day but I pushed forward. I feel you need that in this role because there will be days when you feel like you want to quit. I also asked for help as I knew I was not an expert and found myself being more efficient because of asking for help.

"On day three, I learnt that you have to value yourselves correctly and walk away from deals if they are not a good fit for you. I believe this is vital for this role in sales."

Ian paused before he continued. "And on day four, I felt humbled. I had judged people I worked with incorrectly. I believed that I was better educated and above my co-workers.

I am ashamed of myself for judging them that way as I was always taught to never judge a book by its cover. I also learnt that everyone has tough journeys and my journey so far is nothing compared to others. I will never forget those lessons.

"At the end of the first week, I learnt a valuable skill in leadership. The CEO of the company cared about his employees; he wanted to learn about them out of work and treated them equally.

"When my second week started, I learnt that everyone makes mistakes but to be honest about it, you have to own it and find ways to fix it. Then I learnt about reviews. I know your company has also had some negative reviews so I'm sure you will appreciate this: there will be fake reviews, you can not please everyone but let your work do the talking." Ian paused again.

"At my last assignment, I learnt so much. First I was taught the importance of having a plan to successfully achieve goals, to delegate and be efficient. Then we had to roll up our sleeves and put in extra hours and I'm guessing there will be times where I will have to do that here. I also learnt to treat every customer the same and, finally, I learnt that if you work hard you will be rewarded." Ian paused one last time and smiled.

"Now, in answer to your other question, I got an interview here today because your CEO is Peter Barnes and last week I painted his house. He was so impressed with my work, with the effort I put in and the teamwork I displayed that when I was talking to him he asked me to come for an interview here."

The room was uncomfortably silent for a long time, before Ian did something that surprised both him and the interviewer – he stood up. "Thank you for your time today, but this is not for me." The interviewer shook his hand and stammered, "To be clear, you are walking out of an interview at this firm, one of the best graduate jobs in the city." Ian calmly replied, "Yes. You see, a wise man once taught me that you should not accept a job unless it ticks all three of the following.

1. You have to be passionate about the company. Can you wear their t-shirt with pride and tell your grandad about it? I really love this company, but I'm cautious about the culture.
2. You have to be passionate about the job. I wanted this job because it was a cool job my friends had, but having thought about it I am not sure I will enjoy the role.
3. You have to be passionate about your boss. Is this person going to teach you new things, help get the best out of you? I believe in being honest, I am not sure you

will enhance my career and if you treat everyone like you treated me today I can't see me being happy."

With that Ian walked out and went to his grandad's office, where everyone smiled at him and his grandad handed him the paintbrush.

The Wedding Planner

There was no doubt about it, Pearl Goldberg was the best wedding planner in the city. However you measured it – number of new clients, revenue generated, high-end clients, reputation, number of weddings a year – she was always at the top. She had a legacy in the industry and had done so for the past 10 years. She was in her early fifties and just 5ft 2in. But despite her height, she had a reputation for owning any room.

Brooke had yearned for the opportunity to work for her and it was finally here. All her life, Brooke had wanted to be a wedding planner. She'd put pillowcases on her head as a child pretending to be a beautiful bride at her perfect wedding. She would even boss her friends around as they acted out weddings she'd planned. Now, she was getting her chance at her dream job working for Pearl.

Brooke idolised Pearl. She subscribed to wedding planning magazines, attended wedding events, and followed Pearl for a very long time. She'd been offered a temporary role for just under a year, and Brooke knew she had to grab the opportunity. She knew fate and luck had played a huge part in her getting this job, but sometimes life throws you opportunities, and you have to take them.

Pearl's assistant had just had a baby and had wanted to take a career break. Brooke had been part of a mass layoff from her technology sales role. She had seen the job to be Pearl's assistant and had immediately applied, sending a video to Pearl to show her interest. She did this to stand out from the rest of the candidates. Then, when Brooke's cousin used Pearl for her wedding, Brooke ensured she introduced herself after the ceremony. Pearl decided to give her a chance for the next 12 months.

It was the first week in January and Brooke was ready to go. She arrived at Pearl's office at exactly 8am. The first lesson of the day, she thought, is to wear warmer clothes to the office. The second lesson that she very quickly realised was that the job of the wedding planner was not just during a wedding season but throughout the entire year. Pearl walked into the room and after the pleasantries were completed, she pulled over a massive whiteboard on wheels. At the top of the blank board, she wrote FORECAST; a little below on the right-hand side and slightly off-centre, she wrote LO; then on the far right-hand side, she wrote TARGET.

Brooke was confused and Pearl could clearly see it. "You're wondering why I wrote the things on the right-hand side?"

"Yes, exactly," Brooke responded.

"Regardless of whether you become a wedding planner or whatever job you do, planning is essential and you always start with where you want and need to be. LO stands for 'lights on'. This is the minimum needed to keep the business going. Let's say you're a tech salesperson like you were before you came here," explained Pearl. Brooke laughed. She had been a tech salesperson for a financial services startup before she'd joined Pearl – and she'd been awful at it. In her defence, the company had given her three days of onboarding and then she was left mainly to her own devices, with her manager continuously saying, "Just do as the others do".

Pearl continued, "Regardless of tech sales, running your own business, or doing a role for a big company like a data analyst, you always need to think about what you need to do to keep the lights on. If you run your own business like me, you need to think about how much money you need to keep the business going; in other roles, you need to think what the minimum you need to do is in order to keep your job. The second point is that we should always be thriving to do more than the minimum. Life happens, unexpected things happen, and you always want to strive to do more."

Brooke had been in Pearl's company for 20 minutes and was already mesmerised by her. She was learning so much. "So, what are your magic numbers?" Brooke asked. Pearl smiled and started writing. Under LO she wrote $180k and 30. "Based on the current rent, my expenses, including yours and my salary, inflation etc, I need to generate $180k this year. I make roughly $6k per wedding, so I need to do 30 weddings to keep the lights on. Make sense?" Brooke nodded.

"OK, so let's use some maths here: what do you think our target should be?"

Brooke paused for a moment, "I think we should shoot for 25% over as a target so $225k or 38 weddings." It was Pearl's time to smile. "Sounds great," and then she wrote down BHAG right at the end of the board. "This stands for "Big Hairy Audacious Goal." It's a term used by investors, no idea why. However, it's the goal which, if all the stars align, we can achieve. I think we go for $300k or 50 weddings. We shoot high and see where we land," Pearl said with a smile. "Why not go for $400k?" Brooke asked. "Ah, better to underpromise and overdeliver than the other way around. My grandma taught me that," Pearl replied. "But who are we promising, it's your own business?" Brooke replied. "Well, again, I act as if I have a board of investors just in case I do one day and I also set myself realistic goals so that I'm not disappointed so much that I want to quit if things don't go my way," was Pearl's response.

Pearl bought over a second whiteboard and wrote the words PIPELINE on top. She then drew down several columns titled: Clients, Services, Expected Revenue, and Date. She then filled in the board.

Clients	Services	Expected Revenue	Date
Davis/ Casey	Band, location, photographer	$7k	Feb 14th
Nelly/ Gunner	Location	$8k	March 1st
Greenaway/ Ford	Band, location, photographer, videographer	$8k	March 2nd
Botero/ Speers	Band, location, photographer, videographer, invites, flowers, catering, decor	$12k	March 31st
Stephens/ Visscher	Location and catering	$5k	April 29th
Patel/Patel	Location, music, entertainment	$5k	May 6th
Friedman/ Barnes	Band, photographer, videographer flowers,	$8k	June 29th
Zaltzman/ Malk	Band, location, photographer, videographer, invites, flowers, transportation, catering, decor	$40k	Sept 3rd
Cottis/ Robinson	Photographer, videographer, catering	$6k	Sept 4th

"This is your number-one job for the next year. Every week we're going to review this pipeline board and every day you're going to update it. You know the targets, and as you learn from me, you'll see how we track and what we need to do. What are the first things you notice?" asked Pearl. Brooke paused, looked at the whiteboard and then said. "Well, there are only nine on the board and LO needs 30, but the total revenue is $110k so our deal size is higher than expected. We have to get a lot more clients on this board if we are to achieve BHAG."

"Spot on," Pearl beamed. "There are always three levels to consider here when we smash our target this year. First, is the top of the funnel. The more weddings we have in the pipeline, the more chances we have of hitting goals. Second, deal size. If our average deal size increases, then we won't need as much at the top of the funnel. Third, is the win rate. As I said earlier, life happens. We won't win all of those deals, but the more we can secure, the easier our job becomes." Brooke was writing down notes after notes. "We better get to work then, our first client is in half an hour," Pearl said, smiling at Brooke.

Brooke spent the next week taking in vast amounts of information as Pearl went through everything with her. She had wondered why the prices were different per couple and soon found out that Pearl's whole business was built on relationships, and she got a fee for booking each component.

But, it was important to balance that with what the clients wanted. For example, the Nelly/Gunner wedding really wanted their venue to be a country club, so Pearl got a nice fee but had to negotiate for food, whereas the Davis/Casey wedding was going to be low-key at a restaurant, and for this she got a lower fee. Pearl had relationships with everyone and she had to connect all the dots. Being a wedding planner was tough. She had to set proper expectations with clients and tell them when they needed to raise their budget or lower their demands. She also had to negotiate with the vendors.

The next Monday, Brooke walked in the office and Pearl simply said, "Tell me where we are against our goals." Brooke was nervous about this but had taken a ton of notes throughout the week. "OK. Let's start with the fact that last week we had nine couples and now we have seventeen potential couples," Brooke explained. She went through the names of all the new couples.

"Let me correct you," Pearl said. "We should have 15 on the board. The Friedman/Barnes wedding won't happen." Brooke looked confused. Pearl continued, "I've been around long enough to know that they won't get married."

"But how?" Brooke asked. Pearl's answer: "In wedding planning or other businesses, you have to forecast accurately and to do that you have to read the signs. Their body language and tone on the phone seemed like they are not ready to get married and, add to the fact they have yet to decide on anything, including a venue, which I have told them will take months to book. I just can't see it happening." Brooke was taken aback by everything she had just heard. It made sense but they'd verbally agreed to work with them and she just assumed that was that. "I told you we won't win them all," Pearl said with a grin.

Pearl continued. "The Cottis/Robinson wedding is not going to happen either. Well it is, but they are not going to use us."

"But they said they were keen to work with us," Brooke replied.

"If everybody who said they were interested in me actually became clients, I would already be sipping margaritas on a beach somewhere," Pearl smiled. "They are never going to sign. I suggested some good packages to them within their budget, but they had their heart set on other venues and experiences. Another wedding planner will promise them everything they want and say it's achievable within their budget. They will run over budget later on. They will resent the other wedding planner and never refer them for any other business, but it will be too late to change by then."

Brooke felt disheartened. But she remembered this was a learning experience and she was still taking it all in. They had also increased the pipeline list a bit. The meeting ended and Pearl reminded Brooke of the goals. "If everything on the board actually happens then we can probably keep the lights on but we can't rely on that. We need to hustle all the time."

Brooke was amazed at the effort Pearl put in over the next week. She met a ton of new clients who had been referred to her. The majority of her business came from referrals. However, she was clear to Brooke that if you rely solely on referrals, you will likely miss your goals. Brooke and Pearl had attended a wedding expo conference that was three hours away. "There could be clients here. Even better – a client that wants their wedding in the city. City weddings usually have a larger budget and more amenities," Pearl had told her. She was of course right and they soon had a new couple interested in her services. Pearl also called, emailed and visited new vendors, especially hotels to try and build relationships that would lead to more referrals. She even looked at the local newspapers for engagement announcements and then found the couple on social media and sent cold outreach messages to them. All of these approaches yielded more potential customers.

Over the next few weeks, life continued at full throttle for Brooke and Pearl. When they were not prospecting they were busy doing the wedding planning side of the job, which was exactly what Brooke had imagined the role would be and the part she absolutely loved. Pearl had a reputation for hosting amazing weddings but the work behind the scenes was intense. The Davis/Casey wedding took place this past weekend, and it was the attention to detail that stood out the most. An example of this was that Pearl was in charge of hiring the band. She had called in one of the wedding bands she knew, but had had four conversations with them about songs, when to host strategic breaks, the first dance, how they were getting to the location and so on. Of course the band had turned up early, been a huge success and because of her relationship with them, she got a new lead for another wedding. She was always managing relationships and always asking for referrals. Pearl had also forecast that wedding to be within $100 of exactly how much revenue they would make from it. Brooke was amazed with the results and how important accurate forecasting was.

Brooke loved everything about this job but she did occasionally miss the camaraderie she had previously had with her old work colleagues. It seemed to be all work with Pearl, especially to begin with. However, the onion layers were slowly peeled back, and Brooke got to know more and more about Pearl as a person as they built a great relationship. They became more than just work colleagues. They became friends. After a very long evening at one wedding, Pearl poured Brooke a glass of wine from a bottle gifted to her from the mother of the bride. Brooke had been desperate to ask Pearl some questions and finally piped up: "How did you get into this business and how did you end up running your own business?" Pearl sipped her wine and breathed in. "I loved weddings, but I actually started my career in the event industry. I worked for a global bank that did all the operations for massive events. At first I loved it. Travelling around the world was exhausting, but at the same time, a lot of fun. I did that for nearly 20 years and, through ups and downs, became good at organising and hosting events. But then I started to feel uncomfortable at work. At the time I denied it to myself and others but, reflecting now, I was being bullied and it was horrid.

There were two others on the team as event coordinators and then a manager. The manager who hired me was great and a lot of what I am teaching you I learnt from them. However, they left and the new manager came in and it all changed. To this day, I'm not sure why she treated me as she did. She removed responsibilities from me for no reason, refused to provide feedback, and spoke negatively about me to my peers causing a 'pile-on' culture. I felt alone. I cried myself to sleep and I felt really worthless. I thought about quitting and doing a completely different career but I looked myself in the mirror one day and said, 'Enough is enough'. I worked on knowing my self-worth and that I'm good at what I do – planning events."

Pearl took another sip and continued "At the same time, my daughter was getting married and I thought to myself, 'I can plan her wedding. I love weddings and am a great event planner!' I planned it really well and loved every step of it. I knew these were the types of events I wanted to do. I got a job like you have working for a well-regarded wedding planner and after many years when she was retiring, I decided to venture out on my own. I never looked back and I vowed to never treat anyone how I was treated, and to continuously believe in myself. Whenever I reflect on all of my experiences, I'm grateful for what happened as everything is a learning experience. The scars make you stronger." Brooke had tears in her eyes. Pearl had been completely vulnerable to her and that made her even more inspired. "Wow," she simply said, "thanks for sharing. Cheers to self belief!" and they clinked their glasses.

Brooke's next few months were a complete blur. It seemed every week they were working long hours ensuring at least one wedding went off without a hitch. Some weeks they had three weddings happening. Those were particularly exhausting for Brooke, but she was loving every minute of it. The job itself was exactly what she wanted to do and expected, but it was the additional learning that she knew she could use in most jobs that she loved the most. Every Monday she presented the pipeline and went from asking questions and being nervous to confidently predicting their season.

As her last day approached, Brooke was determined to stay in the wedding planning business. Her contract was ending with Pearl as wedding season had officially come to a close but, as of yet, she had not found a new job. She went into the office one day and Pearl was not there. That's weird Brooke thought and then she saw a bottle of tequila on her desk with a note. She opened it.

Brooke,

I'm off to sip margaritas on the beach for a much-needed vacation. You have what it takes to be the next big wedding planner. When I return, I would love to discuss what I think our future could look like in this business together. Can you hold off on being swooped up by another planner until then?

See you soon, Pearl

PS You can plan all you want but sometimes there are things you can not forecast or predict that will completely change your strategy, this is one of those.

Brooke smiled and then pulled up the whiteboard.

The Lemonade Stand

Jamie was nervous. She liked being in her comfort zone. She liked being in control. She was definitely not in her comfort zone, and she wasn't sure about being in control right now either. She breathed in deeply, got her cup of tea, called her dog, Sox, into her office, adjusted her camera and hit the login button to join the video conference. Today was her first day as a sales manager for a start-up, and she was going to manage six salespeople.

She had interviewed for this role after being turned down for a promotion to a management position in her previous company. It was a perfect timing scenario. While she was trying to get over how she had been rejected, a recruiter had reached out and asked her to interview for this new sales manager role. She'd loved coaching the new hires and sharing her success in her former position, so this felt like a natural move.

She'd been with her previous company for five years and had been a consistent top performer for the whole time that she'd been there. She'd won awards, gone to President's Club and hit targets, so she felt that it was time she got a promotion. She was really disheartened and upset when she found out that she had been overlooked for a colleague who had apparently done more management training. She thought it was a terrible decision. The person who got the job had many complaints against him. He'd also performed at a lower level than Jamie. But, he was friends with the other male leaders and hung out with them socially. While Jamie could never prove it, she felt like this played a huge factor in the company's decision to promote him. Some things happen for a reason, though.

She had completed five interviews all of which had been really productive, and now she found herself starting a new role at a new company. Her new boss had been really welcoming but also very upfront and honest. The sales team had not been performing and he needed her to turn it around so they could secure additional funding.

It was time for her to meet the team and take on this new challenge. She logged in to the video call and was impressed that all her team members were already on the call, and they were all smiling. Abby, one of her team, started the conversation: "We are so excited to work with you," and that made Jamie feel so much better. However, by the end of the day, Jamie was stressed again.

She liked the people on her team, they seemed keen but they were failing and failing badly. It was halfway through the first quarter and the team were not even at 10% of their combined goal. Some of the team had not closed a single deal. She left her final call of the day, did the usual HR onboarding process and shut her laptop. She ordered takeout, poured herself a glass of wine and then opened up her laptop again. She started to read through the notes in their system for all the deals in the team's pipeline. Jamie was a pipeline queen. Ever since her first role, she put detailed notes in on every lead, customer and very opportunity. She was organised with her follow-ups and made sure her emails were all aligned. A manager told her once, "If you win the lottery and don't show up for work the next day, I need to be able to pick up the pieces no problem." That had stuck with her. Plus, she realised she was able to close more deals and build relationships with customers by jotting down all the notes. "You are the only salesperson who remembers my daughter's name," one prospect had told her.

Things were different at this company. There were deals listed with a 75% chance of closing for this quarter but they had hardly any notes in the deal and no follow-up task scheduled with the potential customer. As she scrolled through all the deals, she started thinking there was no way her team would hit targets.

The next few days gave her even more anxiety. Her boss was convinced that their product was great and sales should be better than they were. Marketing had informed her that they had generated more than a thousand leads and they were disappointed that some had been cast aside without much or any interaction from sales. Then, after Jamie had completed her 1:1s with all of the team, she realised that they did not seem to know what to do. Jamie felt out of her league and was really down. Of course, she'd had bad weeks and even months in sales, everyone had, but this was completely new for her.

She decided to text the person who could always cheer her up, her grandad, Gary. Gary was in his eighties and not used to new technology, but he'd recently learnt how to text, to ensure that he could reply to his grandchildren. When Jamie texted him, he instantly replied. He could tell Jamie was struggling with her new role from the text she had sent, and so he invited her to meet him for brunch the next day.

As soon as Jamie arrived, she cheered up. Gary was waving at her in the old diner where they went all the time. "I've already ordered your favourite omelette," he said as they hugged and sat down. "So tell me what's been going on with the new role?" he asked. Jamie went through her week and Gary calmly listened to everything. Jamie felt glad to be talking it through with him. He'd been a travelling salesman for many years, selling refrigeration parts throughout the midwest of America, so he could relate and understand the problems she faced.

Once she finished telling him, he smiled at her. "Well, first things first, I'm glad I'm retired. I have no idea about these systems you have to log calls and emails, I just had a notepad.

However, I think you need to train your team on the basics." Jamie knew that to be true and was wondering if Gary had been the wrong person to ask advice from. Gary almost read her mind. "How did you learn to sell?" he asked. Jamie replied, "When I graduated and started at DeerStone Inc." "That's not true," Gary interjected, "you learnt to sell from the best salesperson in the Midwest, when you were a little girl. Don't you remember the lemonade stand and CHAMPS?"

Of course, Jamie realised that Gary had been her first sales teacher. Every summer he had set her and her sisters a task: build a lemonade stand and make as much money as they could. But then the kicker was to report back on CHAMPS. The winner got a cheesy trophy of a lemonade stand that Gary had created. Jamie won every year and as the memories came flooding back, she knew exactly what to do. She thanked Gary for brunch, went home and was busy preparing for the following week.

Monday morning Jamie was ready for her team meeting. She'd prepared slides and she knew exactly how to deliver her message. The team all logged in to the virtual call and appeared energetic for the week. After the pleasantries, Jamie got straight to the point. She said, "I want you all to learn CHAMPS," as she shared her screen. "It stands for:

- **C**hallenge – What challenge is the customer or prospect facing right now?

- **H**ow – How are they currently trying to solve that challenge?
- **A**uthorities – Who is involved with any decision around purchasing? Who are all the stakeholders?
- **M**oney – Can they pay for what you are selling? What are you charging them? Are they aware of the costs
- **P**roblems – What problems do you face as a salesperson?
- **S**o why now – Why are they going to buy from you right now?"

Jamie repeated it. Then, before they could start asking questions, she carried on: "Today I want you all to cancel your plans. I want everyone to go and create a pop-up lemonade stand. It can be anywhere you want, but you have to report back tomorrow on what you did with CHAMPS as a guideline. I want you to tell us about how much money you spent, what profit you made and anything else of interest."

Everyone stared in bewilderment, thinking she was joking. Jamie anticipated this. "I am not joking – this is how I learnt sales. and as well as a team-building exercise, I think we can all learn from each other. Oh, and one more thing, there is a prize for the winner," and with that she showed them a trophy of a lemonade stand, similar to the one she had won from Gary as a child. She hung up and exhaled, she hoped this would work.

The next morning, she was really nervous. Had they done the homework? Had the experiment worked? She clicked on the scheduled call and everyone was beaming. OK, here goes she thought. "Alright, who wants to go first?" she said. Everyone eagerly raised their hands and Jamie picked on the rep at the top left on her screen, Ben.

"This was really fun," said Ben. "I'm in Arizona, but I don't have a ton of money. However, I spent about $25 on lemons and sugar and had an old fold-down table so I used that to create my lemonade stand in the local park. I made four large jugs, each of which could produce 10 glasses. As for CHAMPS, I felt the *challenge* was that it's hot as hell here and people needed a nice glass of Ben's Lemonade. The *how* was the several convenience stores and ice cream shops already in the park and also that many people had their own water bottles. I felt people might want a change from the norm. As for *authorities*, many of the people are parents who ultimately sign off, but the children are actually the decision makers or certainly the influencers. One little girl begged her mum for lemonade so much that bought two glasses from me. On to *money*. I decided to undercut the local vendors and charge $1 a glass. One *problem* I had was that I didn't plan correctly. I could only carry four jugs and I only packed 40 cups and, of course, dropped two on the floor so I could only sell 38. Finally, *so why now*? Again, it's Arizona and it's hot so everyone needs a drink. After a couple of discounts I made $34 gross, $9 net."

Everyone on the call started clapping and Jamie thought to herself, "This is working!"

"Hajra, you're next," Jamie chimed in after the clapping stopped. "Well, I'm in Washington, D.C. so I didn't have the warm weather like Ben," the audience laughed. "I had a different tactic. I'm originally from Pakistan, and we have a very close community here. My uncle runs a mini-mart that many of my fellow countrymen and women shop in, so I went to visit him. He had lemons and sugar, which I purchased from him for a discount and then set up my shop within his shop.

As for CHAMPS, well, my *challenge* is that many Pakistani people who frequent his store speak Urdu as their primary, if not only, language. A lot of people from Pakistan love fresh drinks and my uncle can only order so much from larger companies. *How* are they doing it now?" she continued. "Simply, they buy from my uncle's shop or a handful of other shops if they are on the shelves or else they make it themselves at home. *Authorities?* The women in the household normally make the decisions around shopping for food and drink but in our culture trust and loyalty plays a very important role. We had numerous people come into the store who have been shopping with my uncle for years, and they simply trusted his recommendation to try my lemonade. *Money* is really interesting. I spent a total of $15, but I charged $2.50 a serving. I didn't do any sort of discount as I felt it wasn't needed. I sold 18 glasses over the day, so I made $45 gross and $30 net. The biggest *problem* I faced was that I had used all of my uncle's lemons by 1pm, so I was forced to shut down my operation. I also had the problem that many people shop in his store because they can communicate in their native tongue. I don't speak Urdu frequently, so communication was a challenge. *So why now?* Monday happened to be a busy day at the store but people simply liked something new that was recommended by a trusted source (my uncle)," she finished. The whole video conference clapped.

Shelton was next. "I actually struggled with this," Shelton started. "I live on the south side of Chicago and although I've lived here all my life, I didn't feel comfortable going out on the street to sell lemonade. It's just not that type of neighbourhood. I also struggled with this idea, being honest. I thought it was childish at first." That took Jamie by surprise. She was going to pipe in in defence, but stopped herself as she appreciated the honesty. Shelton continued, "However, as you all know the most important thing for me is my four-year-old daughter Mia, and I thought maybe this was an opportunity for us to bond. I called her daycare and asked if I could do this at their school and they gladly accepted. Many of the kids there live in my neighbourhood and have also never had a lemonade stand. That was the *challenge*. The *how* is that families in the neighbourhood and the daycare stick together and we try to make sure everyone is OK, so every kid has food and drink but making lemonade is something you do on your own. The *authorities* here, like Ben, were the parents and children. My daughter certainly made all the decisions on that day." The call burst into laughter. Shelton's daughter Mia was adorable and at that point he had brought her into the call to say hi. Once she left he continued. "The *money* piece here was interesting. I went to the local supermarket and told them what I was doing and they gave me 100 lemons and a ton of sugar for free. The school lent me a table and set me up by the entrance. Mia and her class made the signs, so the cost was zero. We did a pay-what-you-want model, and collected $92. All the money went back to the school." There was a moment of silence, and the rest of the team were really impressed with both the amount sold and the generosity. "On to the *problem*. Well, I had to make a lot of lemonade and much though Mia was part of the team, she decided that dressing up and playing was more fun, so I struggled to make lemonade quickly enough! Finally, *so why now*. Simply put, those kids needed the smiles and the school desperately needed the money and the parents needed the best lemonade in Chicago."

Jamie was truly loving this experiment. Not only because they were learning CHAMPS, which she hoped would be helpful for them, but because they were bonding with each other. "Abby, you are next up".

Abby had actually made her virtual background a lemonade stand on the screen and that instantly set the scene. Abby was the most bubbly amongst them and started with, "OK, time for the best story," which bought some smiles. "So let me tell y'all, I am in Atlanta and like Ben it's beautiful and hot down here. I am one of those freaks that loves working out, so I went to my local gym at peak time with my old tailgating table. The *challenge* was simple. Everyone needs a drink to hydrate after a workout. The *how* was also simple: people bring their own drink to the gym. Let's be fair, water is boring or they pay extortionate amounts for a sports drink at the gym. *Authorities*. Well, the gym did have to approve my being there and I had to use my charm for that one but the decision-makers were the people going to the gym. What really helped was a spin teacher promoting my stand after the class." Abby breathed and Jamie could tell under her confidence she was actually a little nervous.

"*Money*. OK, so I went to the supermarket and spent $40 on the ingredients and I charged $2 a cup because the sports drinks were a little more than that. The biggest *problem* I had was that no one had cash at the gym so I had to accept IOUs and then get people to send me the money but I did make $84 and still have three people yet to pay me. The *so why now* is the same as the challenge, they need to hydrate." Again the crowd clapped and Jamie was caught thinking that a problem in sales all the time is customers actually paying.

Garrett went next. "My wife is a nurse at the hospital and she constantly complains about the cafeteria, so I thought I would put my stand there and tackle the *challenge* of the options within the cafeteria. The *how* is also the cafeteria at the hospital, which is run down, in the basement and really expensive. Oh, and they often run out of supplies. But this is the only place where most of the hospital workers go to eat and drink so my thought process was that this really a no-brainer for people. The *authorities* tie in with the *problem* so I'll come back to that later. The decision-makers were patients, staff and anyone using the cafeteria, and my assumption was this was a no-brainer. Unless patients needed certain measured ingredients, people loved the change. However, the biggest *problem* (and linked with *authorities*) was that the operations team at the hospital had to approve me being there and even then I had to make sure I met hygiene rules, such as wearing gloves and a mask. It took a good hour or so for approval. *Money* was similar to everyone. I went to the supermarket and bought the ingredients for about $40 and had no clue on pricing so I charged $1.50, and just about broke even. The *so why now* ties in with what I discussed. I should add one thing, I timed this badly. I went there when my wife started her shift at 1pm, after dealing with the *authorities*, I started selling at about 2.30pm. By that point the cafeteria was empty. I stayed until my wife finished around 8pm, but the 5pm rush was for patients only, many workers only used the cafeteria in the morning or at lunch. *So the why now* should have been 'when' and I should have set up to cover the earlier shifts."

The session ended. Jamie made a glass of lemonade and sipped it outside while watching the sun set. Today had been productive; if nothing else, it had brought the team together. She just hoped it would work.

It didn't take long for things to turn around. CHAMPS had become a 'thing' in her team and also in other departments around the company. Every 1:1 meeting Jamie had with team members now incorporated CHAMPS. They would anticipate what she wanted. "I uncovered a problem, can we brainstorm?" Garrett would say. Or Shelton would start a meeting with, "I've got the customers' *challenge* and how they are doing it but we need to find the *authorities' piece*."

At the end of the year when they'd all achieved their targets and were celebrating at a party they all raised a glass with lemonade.

The Car Dealership

Glyn was a seasoned car salesman, he'd been doing it since he was 17. School had never been his strong suit. While others around him at school could concentrate and develop new skills, he was too easily distracted. As many of his classmates in England had done, he left school at 16. He had low grades and had no clue what to do with his life. He knew he could work hard if someone gave him a chance but so many overlooked him simply because of his grades. Luckily, his dad's friend had given him a job in his car dealership.

He started out as a valet, picking up keys and parking cars, running errands and washing cars – washing a lot of cars! He had done that for a couple of years and firmly believed that hard work and grit had helped him get to where he is today. Any new employee he's hired has had to wash cars for their first month of employment, too, regardless of title or experience. His CFO was mortified when he was informed of this during their interview. He was in his sixties and had been an accountant for many years. However, he was a great sport about it saying afterwards that he had a new appreciation for the term 'squeaky clean'. It had also helped him see the ins and outs and appreciate every aspect of the business. Glyn had also fired several employees over the years for not taking this seriously.

After doing the hard graft for the first few years, Glyn moved into a customer support role. From there, he was taught about the mechanics and service department. As part of the business focused on high-end premium cars, Glyn learnt that the service had to be exceptional. After that role, his career took another change and he moved into sales. He was naturally great at sales and went on to be the lead salesperson there for 20 years. Eight years ago, his friend's dad decided it was time to retire and Glyn purchased the business from him. Today, Glyn is the proud owner of Exquisite Cars and Motors plus Essential Cars – his second more economy-friendly dealership.

When Glyn started, the company consisted of just one dealership, Exquisite Cars and Motors, so it was a huge gamble to diversify the business into new markets. But Glyn was always one to take a chance. He estimated that only around 2% of the population of England could afford one of the cars from his premium dealership, however, Glyn knew first-hand that there was a much bigger market out there.

His mum had been a teacher and his dad worked in a paper pressing factory all his life. They couldn't afford luxury cars. They could barely afford a car at all. That had motivated him throughout his career. He had always wanted to make cars available for everyone and so Essential Cars was created.

He was really proud of his businesses, the results they had driven and the reputations they had built. They were located about 30 miles from London. It was a middle-class area but, like any town, it had some rougher and some nicer areas. As a result of his hard work over the years, he had built a nationally recognised brand, based mainly on its reputation for honesty and support. People from all over the UK came to them to buy their luxury cars. But people from all over London and the surrounding area came to Essential Cars for their economy cars as well, despite the competition. Essential Cars was in the top 20 dealerships in the UK for both revenue and cars sold.

Each year, he had one favourite day – it was the day the secondary school children came to the car dealership for a day of work experience. He liked to give work experience to the kids at the same school he'd attended. He knew there were others struggling academically at school like he had but that they could still be a success. He wanted to show them this.

These kids were all about 16 or 17 so seeing lots of high-end sports cars was exciting for them. Glyn, however, hoped that he could teach them some important skills, both in life and, potentially, in sales if they took that route. He despised the view that car salespeople were sleazy and always looking for a quick sale. Of course, there were those types in the industry who would sell a second-hand car that wouldn't last one journey but he was sure the same could be said about salespeople in any industry.

He had recently become upset after a technology company that boasted all over the internet about how honest and great they were had completely mis-sold him on a recruitment tool. He found out after the sale was completed that he could have got everything he needed for 30% less than he paid. When he complained about this, the company was not interested in hearing it or doing anything to fix it. As he thought about this it made him angry, but he reminded himself that this was why he liked doing the exercises he planned for today. Honesty in business is crucial if you want to gain and, more importantly, keep customers.

Glyn had put a lot of time into organising the day's event. The kids arrived and he'd set up a buffet breakfast for them in the staff cafeteria Exquisite Cars and Motors. There were 16 kids in total and by default the tables had four chairs each so they were instantly split into four teams.

"Good morning everyone," he began, smiling. "I am so excited to have you visit our businesses today. I started working here when I was your age. I wasn't very good at school and my first lesson is that that's OK. Some of you may study for the next seven years, and that is also OK. You have to follow the right path for you. Hopefully some of the things you learn today you can use on any path." Glyn paused. "My team and I worked extremely hard to get to where we are as a dealership today. I own one of these cars," he said, pointing to a red Italian sports car. "I have a comfortable home with no mortgage. I go on holiday twice a year and I can always buy my round at the pub. When I was your age, I didn't think I could get where I am or achieve any of that. I grew up on the rough side of town and several of my school friends are either in or have been in jail. I got my lucky break here, but even then there have been tough times. My hard work has got me where I am." There was pause, the room was silent with the exception of a few gasps. Glyn had done this exercise and speech for the last seven years and every time he got the same response.

"The second lesson is that in life, it's important to learn about tone, body language and perception. People can lie, people can mislead and people can manipulate you and the more you can read people the better you will be. Today I want you to *read* both of the dealerships along with my team. Don't worry, you will all get to spend time at Exquisite and touch the very fancy cars but you'll also spend time at Essential as I want you to see the way we operate both businesses. There are a lot of similarities on how we operate and there are naturally some big differences. My team and I will give you feedback, but we will see how well you do in sales. I've split you into four departments – red, blue, black and yellow. These will be your teams. You'll find your colour on the table, and my team will guide you throughout. At the end of the day, I want you to share your stories. Sounds fun? OK, let's get started."

The children quickly found their colours went off into the dealerships. Glyn sat back and watched the day unfold – from the cameras dotted around, from walking the grounds and from the feedback of others. Glyn bought them back at around 3pm and ordered pizza. While they were all eating he said to the group, "So, what happened?"

"Amazing," said one child from the Black team, "we sold a car."
"Wow, that's great," replied Glyn with a big grin. "Let me hear about it."
"The gentleman came into the Exquisite dealership. We knew he was interested as he knew the brand, knew the specifics of the car, and asked a lot of what we determined as 'buying questions'."
"I still want more information, what were these buying questions? What was his tone and body language like?" Glyn pressed. Several other children from the group interjected. "His tone was passionate. He was really excited about the car. He was telling us how he had recently retired and had been looking at this as a present to himself." Another child said, "I knew he was going to buy it when he asked about the maintenance package you offer and if he could get it checked sooner if required."

"BRAVO!" Glyn shouted. "Questions about maintenance are perfect buying questions as they have already been thinking about the car. Excitement in their tone is a crucial sign for buyers." Glyn looked around, "OK, who's next? How about the Red team?"

One child stepped up. "Well, at first we thought we had lost a buyer and were really upset. Then Andy on your team explained to us how they were never really interested."

"I speak for the room when I say, 'we all want to know more'," Glyn said. "They were dressed in a custom-fitted suit, so we thought they clearly had money and wanted one of your high-end cars. They sat behind the wheel and wanted a test drive, so we again thought they were interested. But, after the drive, their tone was nonchalant and they didn't seem to care. We thought we had messed up by not asking the right sales questions but on reflection, we think they just wanted a test drive and had no interest in buying."

"This is GREAT learning," Glyn boomed. "Let me reiterate that reading tone, body language and controlling perception helps you win in life. You could have spent a lot more time trying to negotiate with them when they were never interested and if you were to have a career in sales you can identify the free-riders quickly now. Hit us Yellow team; tell us your story." A girl from the team stepped forward. "We should have got a sale but, unfortunately, we let them get away." The girl sounded sad but carried on. "Someone came in, he wore ripped jeans and a t-shirt from a high-street brand. We instantly assumed that he couldn't afford a car. When we spoke to him, he was constantly on his phone and didn't seem to care about what we had discussed. He left after about five minutes. We found out later that he is the leading scorer in the Italian football league at the moment and is soon going to be moving to a London team."

Glyn stood up. "First of all, how were you supposed to know he was an Italian footballer? My team can recognise most English players but very few people know all of the footballers from around the world. Second, this is a great example of the importance of tone and body language. I have to tell you, I've probably let a whole football team walk away from this place. If you were to do this again, you will know that perception is important and what they are wearing does not determine who they are. Never judge a book by its cover. It took me a great amount of time learning the art of discovery, how to start conversation and then how to start asking them buying questions. Don't worry, if he's interested he will probably come back and this a great learning experience, thank you for sharing." Everyone in the room clapped.

"OK, let's finish off here, Blue team?"
"We didn't sell a car," one of the girls said with a slightly dejected tone. "But… we got a verbal agreement!" she continued, with a lot more passion and energy. "See what I did there with tone and body language?" and the room all laughed, including Glyn. The girl who was now bustling with energy was a prime example of how tone can capture the moment. She

went on with her story. "We had a lady come into the Essential dealership and she was looking around and browsing. Kerry on your team went up to her and discovered that she is a nurse who needs a new car as her old one just died on her. But when we did further discovery, what we uncovered was that she is nervous about spending so much money on a car. Especially as she is still young and her salary isn't a lot. She had savings set aside for a car and she knew she needed one to drive to work and to visit her family an hour away on the coast.

Kerry was really amazing. She actually told her as part of the conversation that maybe she shouldn't buy the car. I was amazed that a salesperson was walking away from a sale but, because Kerry was so welcoming, the client opened up more and they talked through her concerns almost like friends. She discussed how if she didn't have a car she would have to get transportation. She wouldn't get to see her family and she really missed them and wanted to see them more. Although that helped reassure the customer, she still had doubts. Kerry sat her down with a cup of tea and talked them through with her.

They spoke about how she was not a confident driver and again the customer reiterated how worried she was about the financial side. Kerry told her that there were multiple options and that this was a problem they solved together." She continued, "That was the key. Kerry was genuine and didn't want to sell to her, but rather solve a problem with her. They went through several cars and then Kerry showed her an automatic car that was easy to drive. After the test drive, the client said she would like to come back later with her brother to test it again, but she did want to purchase the car. She had flipped from being really nervous to really excited."

Glyn was clapping and he briefly whispered in Kerry's ear. "Kerry here is one of our top reps. However, 'top' is an interesting term. She doesn't generate the most money for the company as she doesn't sell from the Exquisite dealership. She chooses to sell on the Essential dealership as she believes in helping others less fortunate than her. She is our top rep in terms of cars sold. She is amazing, and that is because she listens and empathises with clients. Did any of you notice that we offer the same snacks, soft drinks and water to everyone regardless of dealership? It is vital we always create the same customer experience. Let me say something that I hope sticks with all of you 'PEOPLE BUY FROM PEOPLE!' There are competitors, and if the cars are the same, the price is similar, the sale is created by the *experience* the customer has and that's down to the salesperson. Kerry's actions were a prime example, as she acted like a consultant not a salesperson and focused on a win-win scenario."

Just as the kids were finishing their pizza and getting ready to go back on the bus, one of the kids shouted, "Look." All the kids and Glyn looked over to see the nurse and her brother were already back at the dealership and talking to Kerry.

In the distance they could also see the Italian footballer, this time with others talking to some of Glyn's staff. "People buy from people," one of the kids shouted. Glyn smiled, today had been a great success. The last kid to get on the bus was the same one who had lost the sale. She paused as she got on the bus and turned to Glyn, "Are you hiring? I loved it here and I really want to work hard and learn from you and your team." Glyn paused for a moment and then beamed, "If you're really interested in working here come back on Saturday and be prepared to wash cars."

"Oh, I'll be here," the girl replied as she boarded the bus.

The Vacation

Almasi's name meant diamond in her native Kenya and right now she felt like the brightest diamond in the whole wide world. "You earned this," kept ringing in her ears. Her boss had said that to her two weeks ago before she had set off on a vacation. It had been a long journey for her but she could hardly believe where she was.

Almasi had grown up in Kenya. Her father was a politician and her mother a nurse, and they lived in a suburb of Nairobi. Almasi had gone to school and was the brightest student in her year, thriving in science and maths. For a long while, she had thought about becoming a doctor, but some of her mother's stories from being a nurse had put her off. More than anything, though, Almasi loved America and longed to visit one day.

Growing up, Almasi loved to watch American TV shows and films, read American books and magazines – she simply loved everything about the USA! Las Vegas and the strip were her number one location, and she dreamt of visiting them. But she also wanted to visit New York, Washington, California and so many other places.

When she turned 18, she knew she wanted to go to university and had the grades to do so. She was set on going to her local university but then a tragedy struck. Her sister and father were killed in a car crash. Almasi was a mess. Her life had been turned upside down; much as her mum and younger brother needed her at home, she wanted to escape. Her local library hosted a career fair and there someone told her about studying in England. She listened intently about the advantages of experiencing a new country and discovered that if she studied a STEM (Science, Technology, Engineering or Mathematics) course her education would be paid for. Science and maths happened to be her best subjects, so she filled in the application form there and then.

The next few months and years were a complete whirlwind for Almasi; she had interviews with several UK universities, all online through her local library. She received several offers from English universities and ultimately decided on studying in Sheffield.

She had researched the city, taken virtual tours and loved everything she had seen. The recruiting team was also a big factor in her decision; they were the friendliest and they jumped on numerous calls just to reassure her. The university and the recruiting team arranged her travel and before she had blinked an eye she was living in the middle of Sheffield studying maths and statistics.

It was while she was in her first year of university that she met Linda. Linda was the opposite of Almasi; she was shy and quiet whereas Almasi wanted to be an American and was loud and funny. They first met when Linda had coached Almasi for a statistics course, and Almasi quickly felt feelings she had never experienced before. In Kenya, same-sex relationships were banned so Almasi suppressed her feelings but now, finally, she was free to be who she was.

They became inseparable and fell in love. Linda was from England and her family had both met and accepted Almasi. On the flip side, Almasi had been nervous to tell her mum and her brother about Linda but, one day over Christmas on a video call, she had plucked up the courage and was surprised at how accepting they were. It felt like a weight had been lifted from her; the anxiety she had endured had crippled her and affected her studies and health.

When they graduated, Linda got into an graduate entry-level role within government. Almasi wanted to stay in England but she needed to find a job and she had no idea what she wanted to do. She randomly saw a job for a graduate sales programme in a technology company and the description seemed ideal – she had an outgoing personality and she was driven, so she hit the apply button.

Once again she found herself caught up in a whirlwind of interviews, including a video interview, one on campus and finally at the company's head office in Manchester. The headquarters were like nothing she had ever seen before. There was cool art on the walls, people playing video games, there was a cafe with free food, and beer on tap. Everyone was really friendly and Almasi knew she wanted to work there. To Almasi's amazement, she got the job and she felt so excited. She would be selling accounting software to hospitals throughout the United Kingdom. "Okay," she thought, "I can do this."

But, as she walked into the office on the first day, she had no idea how she was going to do it and for the first time since coming out to her family, anxiety was eating her up. She sat down with her new boss, Skyler, who she really liked. He had conducted two interviews with her and on both occasions had been really passionate about the role and her potential. He was calm and softly spoken, but clearly knew what he was talking about. The first thing he asked Almasi was, "What's your goal?" Almasi responded, "I want to be successful in this role."

Skyler smiled and laughed a little. "That's great but what is YOUR goal?" Almasi seemed a little confused so Skyler stepped in. "Have you heard of a vision board?" Almasi shook her head. She had no idea what he was talking about. Skyler explained, "Everyone on my team has a vision board, including myself. We put down our goals, what we want to achieve on a personal level and then we hold each other accountable to get there. For example, my current vision board is a car for my wife. She works for a non-profit organisation and is amazing. She's had her car for nine years and never complains. I want to work as hard as possible so that I can help her get a new car this year with the commission I make. I get my commission if we achieve our team goals, which we will. You'll get your commission based on your own performance. Here's why we do that on my team. We work hard, you'll have ups and downs and you will go from ecstatic to despair, sometimes in the same day. That is sales."

Almasi was not sure she liked the description and she was wondering if she had made the right move. As if Skyler could read her mind, he continued: "Whenever you hit a target, you get a nice commission payout. I want you to put some of it towards whatever is on your vision board and create a memory. That way all your hard work will be worth it, and whenever you've a bad moment that memory will stick with you as to why we work hard." Almasi was finally catching up with this idea and it made sense.

"So, let me ask again, what is your goal?" Almasi knew how to answer this time. "As crazy as this might seem, I love America, I love everything about it. I grew up watching American television shows and movies and had plans as a child to visit numerous cities there. I would love to go there one day with my girlfriend, and Las Vegas is high on the list." This time Skyler's smile was huge, "That's a fantastic goal. We're going to get you there and tonight I want you to create a vision board that you can pin in front of your desk."

Almasi spent the evening creating her perfect trip to America, including Linda's input as well. The next day at the office, Skyler called a team meeting and Almasi met her colleagues. Skyler asked the team to go through their vision boards. One of Almasi's team members wanted to put a deposit down on a house, another wanted a motorbike, several, like Almasi, wanted to travel, one wanted a very expensive handbag and another a very nice watch. When the team had completed this exercise, they applauded each other and Skyler said, "Look around you, help each other achieve your goals. You may all have individual aims and targets, but we are a team."

For the first month, Almasi did a lot of training. Skyler reminded her that you have to slow down to speed up: everyone wants to just get going, but the training will help. "We invest in our people here, we put a lot of time into training so you can succeed in your role. Olympic champions don't just go to the finals, they spend years practising and training for the chance to win gold." Skyler had said during their first day. He had also gone on to explain the M.O.S.T onboarding methodology. "We know that onboarding is vital for people's career so we train you on all aspects of the role. Here's what it stands for:

- **M** is for Market. We want you to understand our customers. In our case, it's hospitals and how their accounting team operates. But it's more than that, we will also teach you what struggles they have.
- **O** is for Offering. How do we solve their struggles? What do we offer and what do our competitors offer?
- **S** is for Skills. This is a sales role so we want to teach you sales skills, but there are other essential skills you need to learn to succeed.
- **T** is for Tools. There are a lot of tools you will need to use here to be successful. From tracking your pay to logging the calls you make, and you need to know all of these so they become second nature to you."

Almasi was impressed with the training and was reminded by Linda that they were investing a lot more in her than she was experiencing herself. However, she kept seeing her vision board and wanted to start selling so she could go to America. She was really tempted to book flights now on a credit card but she felt that was cheating, she had to earn the right for the trip. That was the whole point of the vision board and, besides, she didn't want credit card debt on top of her student loan debt, and she didn't know if this job would work out.

After the first month, Almasi was struggling. She was doing everything she had been trained to do; calls, emails, social media; she had been praised by Skyler for her pitch but it just wasn't working and she was bottom of the team. She sat down with Linda one night. "I may have made a mistake with this career. I love everything about this role but I'm not succeeding," she said. Linda simply replied, "Don't give up yet," and hugged her. That's what she needed.

Skyler called her into his office. "Do you like popcorn?" he asked. "Sure," Almasi responded to this weird question. "Follow me," he said, and they ended up in the office kitchen. "To make popcorn you put the oil in the pan and then when the oil starts to heat up, you put the kernels in, or in this case you put the bag in the microwave" he continued while putting a popcorn bag into the microwave.. Where was he going here she thought.

"You studied science right? So you are used to testing theories. Based on this process, all the popcorn should pop at the same time. But they don't, they all pop whenever they want and no one has explained why to me." Almasi knew there were multiple factors as to why; the hull of the kernel and the water content were just two reasons. However, she didn't want to interrupt. "My point being is that I look at everyone on the team like popcorn; you all pop at your own pace. You might be at the bottom now, but you won't be for long." Almasi was so grateful for a great manager like Skyler, who continued to support her.

Three months into the role, something clicked for Almasi; she closed her first hospital. It had been hard work but seeing the email come in with the signed contract, plus a separate email from the customer saying: "Thanks Almasi for being patient with us. This tool is going to be really great for us," made her day and week. Skyler high fived her and printed out a copy of the email, pinning it next to her vision board.

From that moment onwards, Almasi soared. She knew how to work with customers, knew what worked for her and she grew in confidence. Of course, she didn't always hit her target and had setbacks but she learnt to overcome them. At her six month mark, Skyler called her into the office and said, "I have an offer for you. You're doing great and we have a new opportunity – would you like to try and sell our solution into the African market? You can work from here and do the same role, it'll just be a different market. It may be harder as we have never really done anything there." Almasi was honoured to be considered but nervous. It was a new strategy for her but, again, Linda convinced her with simple words: "You got it."

Almasi rocketed in the role. She worked random hours to get hold of people and she had to adapt her tactics a little, but she repeatedly looked at her vision board and kept on going. At the end of the year, she had exceeded her targets and Skyler's team was the number one sales team in the country and number four in the world.

They were all out celebrating when Skyler had opened his laptop up. He called everyone over and told them to fulfil their vision boards. In front of Almasi, her colleagues were clicking online, buying a motorbike or booking an appointment with a mortgage advisor, and then it was her turn. She was hesitant; she had earned good money but was this reckless? Skyler whispered in her ear, "You earned this." She put flights on hold to go to Vegas in a couple of weeks time. Later that night, she surprised Linda. "I've earned this," she said proudly as she was explaining to Linda. That night they planned their whole trip. They'd be starting in Vegas, then onto Orlando, New York and, finally, home.

As she boarded the plane to start her vacation, she heard a voice in her head saying, "You earned this." They landed in Vegas and arrived at the hotel. This time, it was Linda's turn to surprise Almasi. "I made a reservation for dinner and I got a dress for you to wear." They left their room with Linda insisting that Almasi be blindfolded in the lift so she wouldn't know what restaurant they were going to. Cautiously, Almasi did as she was told. As they stepped out of the lift, Linda whispered, "Now take off your blindfold. I love you." Linda was down on one knee, "Will you marry me?" she asked. Almasi broke into tears; she felt like the biggest, sparkliest diamond of all.

The Baker

Pierre was tired. His feet ached a little more often these days and he felt exhausted most nights. He had worked on his feet for six days a week for over 10 years. Of course, it was going to take a toll on him. He took a small sip of wine and said to the woman opposite him, "OK, what do you want to know?"

Ella was a journalist for a national newspaper, with a column and a podcast on unique restaurants in America. She had wanted to interview Pierre for a while, as he owned L'Amore Patissiere in a Denver suburb. It had received over a thousand positive reviews and every time she had done a piece on a restaurant in Denver, people asked, "Is it L'Amour Patisserie?"

Pierre had rejected her requests for a long time with excuses like, "I'm too busy to talk" or "why do I need to talk to a newspaper, I don't need the press?" But finally, his 15-year-old daughter, Matilde, had convinced him to do the interview because she was proud of her dad and insisted people should hear his story. Pierre was in his early forties, but he looked older. He had an impressive aura about him and Ella felt slightly intimidated.

"How did you start the business?" She asked, as she hit the record button.

Pierre took a sip of wine. "I am from France and love fresh baked food. My grandparents owned a patisserie in Lille and I used to help them. I came to Denver to study; it was so beautiful here and I instantly loved it. I met wonderful people, including my wife, and never wanted to leave. However, when I graduated, I struggled to get a job so I started baking and that led me to opening L'Amour Patisserie."

Ella came in with the next questions straight away. "It's rumoured that your business is one of the top-grossing restaurants in the state – do you have plans to expand it to other locations?" Pierre answered with a straight face, "I do not look at records, I stick to my own lane. I am quite sure there is no other French bakery in the area like mine, so my only competitor is myself. I am providing enough money for my family to live comfortably, we travel to France every year and we also go on our own vacation. If I opened a second location, I would lose the uniqueness about L'Amour Patisserie and also the time to have the vacations I love. I don't want that."

His answer was a little blunt and Ella was not warming to her interviewee, but she carried on. "So what makes the restaurant unique?" Pierre responded, "It's a French patisserie run by a French man in Denver, I think that makes us fairly unique. Also, our food is freshly baked with none of the chemicals Americans put in their food."

At this point, Matilde, who had been sitting at the table with her dad and Ella, intervened. "Perhaps, Ella, it would be better to see my dad and L'Amour Patisserie in action; why not spend the whole day with him tomorrow?" Ella paused for a minute. As a journalist, she always went to visit the restaurant and not just take people's word for things, but a whole day seemed a long time.

She had planned to swing by the place in the morning, but something in her gut told her to agree with Mathide's suggestion. "OK. What time do you open?"
"The doors officially open at 7am, but you should arrive about 6am. I promise you the experience will be worth it," was the reply. Again, Ella paused but agreed.
"I have one more question for you tonight, if you don't mind me asking," Ella said as she was getting up to leave. "Of course," Pierre replied. "Why L'Amour Patisserie?"

For the first time Pierre had a massive smile on his face. "L'Amour" means love in France and we are a very passionate nation. Love means multiple things to me. I never wanted to work for a company or person where I didn't love what I do every single day. I feel the same for my employees; I want them to love coming to work every day. In the past when an employee did not love working for us I told them to find their passion. Love grows further than that, though. I also want love from my customers, I want them to love the pastries and food they eat at our place, I want them to enjoy their experience and I want them to feel loved and welcome even if they only visit us once or if they frequent us every day."

"That's amazing," Ella said and she smiled for the first time during the interview. She left and went back to her hotel. All night she kept thinking about what Pierre had said. A lot of restaurant owners said something similar but there was such passion and conviction about the way he explained what his restaurant meant.

Ella woke up early and resisted the urge to get coffee from the hotel as she wanted to try food and coffee at L'Amour Patisserie. She rarely got up this early for anyone but she wanted to see all the restaurant had to offer. She arrived right after 6am. Instantly, she could see that this place was unique. The front looked closed but as soon as she walked in she felt happy.

There was an open kitchen and three staff along with Pierre who were there making croissants and pastries. It smelled amazing and everyone was smiling, even Pierre. He gave Ella the typical French hug and two kisses, and said, "Welcome, I am sorry about yesterday. I was exhausted and I struggle when it comes to talking about my place in a boastful way. Hopefully, you will enjoy today and have a different opinion of me." Ella smiled. Pierre introduced her to the two chefs, Cooper and Taylor, and the front-of-house team member Izzy.

They were all beaming even at 6am, singing to songs and having fun.

Ella quickly discovered they had all worked there for over five years. Cooper wanted to be a chef, but loved baking so much, particularly here. Taylor had gone through a messy divorce and was a mum of two young kids. She loved working at the restaurant because it could fit around her schedule. Finally, there was Izzy. She was a youngster who had started working part-time, while at college and then continued afterwards.

At about 6:20am, Pierre packed up three bags of croissants and headed to the front door. "Bonjour Rebecca! For you." The customer was really appreciative, paying and telling Pierre to keep the change. "I thought you didn't open for another 40 minutes?" Ella said. "That's Rebecca, she's a doctor at the hospital down the road and starts her shift in 10 minutes. She messaged me that some of her colleagues wanted croissants this morning and we made it happen."

"You went out of your way for her?" Ella stammered. "Not really, we are here, she loves the croissants as do her colleagues, and they do great work for the community. They go out of their way more than we do. They were all on the front line during that terrible day with the shooter so It's the least we can do." Ella's memory was jogged to the mass shooting she heard about in this area, but there were a lot of them in America and she didn't remember the details. She asked Izzy about it. "It was awful. This dude started firing just up the road, everyone was screaming. Pierre took as many as could into the storeroom and started baking for everyone." Ella thought how devastating the experience must have been.

Promptly at 7am, the door opened and there was a line of people waiting. In the previous hour, the staff had baked so much that the empty shelves an hour ago were now lined with fresh pastries and food. The smell was amazing and in the back Cooper was continuing to bake.

Izzy came over to Ella and said, "OK, before we get busy, what can I get you?" Ella looked down the menu, it all seemed great. "Is the quiche ready?"
"Of course, we make them every day."
"Then I will have the quiche with ham, please, no salad. Instead, can I have fresh fruit but no pineapple and an almond croissant and a caramel latte with almond milk? Sorry for the complex order." Ella was grateful, as Izzy wrote down her order. She had been to thousands of restaurants and by her guess, only about 50 percent of servers noted the order. This annoyed Ella as it was a simple thing to do. Whenever orders were wrong, it was nearly always from the servers who hadn't written down the orders.

She was seriously impressed a second later when Izzy replied, "OK I just want to get your order right so can I relay this back to you? Quiche with ham, fruit but no pineapple, an almond croissant and caramel coffee with almond milk?" Very few servers reiterated orders and it's the little things like that which make restaurants get great reputations. This was just another sign of how much they cared Ella thought. Izzy was not done though and continued.

"Would you like the almond milk heated for your coffee? Many do but I wanted to double check?"
"Yes please," Ella replied. Once again, she impressed with the attention to detail.
"One more thing," said Izzy, "can I suggest the chocolate almond croissant instead of the regular one. It's a dollar more but it's so worth it."
"Sure," said Ella. As Izzy walked away, Ella started to realise they treated all their customers this way – simply to go above and beyond. She had been 'upsold' but Izzy had done such a good job building trust that it was a no-brainer. She bet that every day they made a good amount of money from upselling products purely from building trust with the customers.

Ella loved her breakfast and spent the morning observing the operation. She could see why everyone loved this place, and she was beginning to love it, too.

When Mrs Harrop came in, Izzy and Pierre both knew her order of eggs and lox and chatted to her for several minutes. She was a retired widow who liked to come into the restaurant to do her crossword. Ella found out that despite Pierre being really busy he sat with her most days. Then there was Mr Schwartz, who was allergic to eggs. Pierre and Cooper had created a quiche with egg substitute just for him, although now others ordered it as well. Then there was John and Cynthia who had started their own consulting business and came there to order almond chocolate croissants. But they sat in an area where they could put up their white board and discuss their strategy. Ella had spoken to them briefly and they had told her how when they started out, Pierre had suggested they use his place as an office rather than renting their own. He had also recommended customers to them, and when they had a bad month with the business, he gave them a tab.

But Ella's mouth almost fell to the ground when two men in suits walked in just before lunch. It had been fairly busy all morning, but by this time had become very busy, so much so that Ella ordered lunch so she didn't feel guilty about taking up a table. The men sat down next to Ella and were rude to Izzy right from the start, something that wasn't unusual in the restaurant industry, Ella knew. But Izzy was remarkably calm and smiled throughout. One of the men asked for the French onion soup but without bread or croutons. Izzy informed the customer that the soup was pre-made with croutons and with the lunchtime rush, they couldn't fulfil his request. Nothing different there, but it was what she said next that was unique. "So if you really have your heart set on a French onion soup, there is a restaurant two blocks from here called The Bagel. It's run by a fabulous guy called Irv and they have French onion soup which they make with croutons on the side. It's not made by a French guy but it's pretty good. Tell them I sent you."

Ella could not believe the transparency. She had taken abuse from a customer and handled it by recommending a competitor. The customer clearly appreciated the honesty, too, and actually decided to stay. Ella suspected this was because of the way Izzy had responded and she watched carefully as the man wolfed down his salad and went back to the line to order a second dessert. Ella overheard him saying, "Thank you for a wonderful experience. I am taking this home for tonight and will definitely come back here."

Throughout the morning and lunch rush, what was clear was that the whole staff did two things:
1. They listened and communicated. Every single customer who walked in had a unique story and unique order and the staff communicated clearly with all of them in an empathetic way. They also communicated with each other to ensure the operation ran smoothly.
2. They were having fun and this place was fun to be at. They had even broken out the happy birthday song and got the whole restaurant singing to a customer called Dotty who was celebrating her 88th birthday.

Ella's flight was at 5pm so a little after 1pm she started to say her goodbyes to everyone. Pierre came up to her. "Thank you so much for coming, I hope you enjoyed it. I was actually wondering if you could run a quick errand with me?" he said. "I have to be at the airport soon," Ella replied.

"It's on the way. I'll take my van, just follow me," he answered.

Reluctantly Ella agreed. There was something about Pierre and this place she couldn't help but like. She followed Pierre. They pulled up in an old people's home and Pierre waved her over. She suddenly realised what was happening. Pierre said, "I wasn't sure about telling you about this because I don't like to promote myself. However, this is part of who we are and we're proud of this. In the afternoon, we deliver any leftovers to one of a dozen places including this place, the children's hospital, a halfway house and a homeless shelter. We figure these people need it more than us and we enjoy baking. Please don't write about this. People should come to us because they like the experience, but we love our community."

Ella boarded her flight and wrote her story passionately on the plane. It was published two weeks later and when Matilde showed Pierre, he smiled. Three months later, Ella happened to be returning to Denver. She booked an early flight so she had time to go to L'Amour Patisserie. As she walked in she was greeted as a friend. Cooper and Taylor hugged her, Pierre gave her a warm welcome and Izzy simply said, "Let me guess, the chocolate almond croissant and the caramel coffee?" Ella simply smiled and said, "Maybe we'll make it two."

The Detective

Mike Gossard looked out of his office window onto the Melbourne harbour. He had a great view; he could see the beaches on one side with the stadium on the other and, in the distance, he could see the cruise ships and the dockyards. It was peaceful up there, which was why he liked it. He had spent too much of his life surrounded by chaos and despair; this was a tranquil moment that he relished.

He had been in the job for 35 years and now it was coming to an end. He could have retired 10 years ago but, deep down, he loved his job so he had delayed and delayed, but now it was time. He had already packed up his desk, completed the necessary paperwork – all he had left was to go to the new recruits' centre and talk to the next generation of police officers. He really didn't want to do this. Why should he? He had given enough but his chief had begged him and the irony was that his daughter, Charlotte, was going to be in the class.

The drive over to the training academy was about an hour but it was a fairly peaceful drive. Mike was gathering his thoughts – what would he say to them, what could he teach them? Like many police officers there was that juggling act between loving the role and hating it. Part of Mike wanted to scare them all, especially Charlotte, and tell them stories of what he had seen, secretly hoping that several recruits might change their mind. Policing had changed as well, it was much tougher now than when he started, much more dangerous. However, he still felt he was doing good; he felt he was getting the bad people off the streets and that was why he had delayed his retirement and why deep down, he loved his job.

He drove round the training facility one last time before parking. He slowly got out of the car and walked in where he was greeted by Captain Ford. "Thank you again for coming."

"Of course," Mike replied. He followed the captain down the hall, got himself a water and took a seat in the middle of a large hall. There were empty chairs circled around him, so he could be seen by everyone. Mike felt like a politician at a town hall, hating all the attention. "Here we go," he thought.

Mike was a humble man who felt he had simply been doing his job over the years, and there were plenty of other cops the same. He wasn't anything special. Captain Ford said he would grab the recruits while Mike went through his notes one more time.

The new recruits bundled in the room and Ford started the proceedings. "Recruits, we are joined tonight by a legend within the Melbourne police force. Lieutenant Detective Mike

Gossard is retiring after 35 years of service. He started here in this same room, went on to be a cop on the beat before taking his detective exams. That led to him being one of the leading detectives to serve this great city. He has solved over 600 murder cases and that includes finding Melbourne's most notorious serial killer who had taken 12 souls." The room clapped and cheered and Mike felt very embarrassed. Ford continued, "Lieutenant Detective Gossard, let's start with what advice do you have for these no recruits?"

"What do you mean, apart from don't sign up?" joked Mike. The crowd laughed. "My biggest advice is to remember that what you are doing is for the greater good. Unfortunately, there are some very bad people out there and your moral compass called you here. There are thousands of jobs out there, but for some reason all of you chose to be here, chose to serve and protect, and chose to do good in this world. Never forget that and remember that what you do makes the world a better place, even if slightly." Mike paused. "I had a whole script planned out here, but I'm not very good at presenting to large crowds so why don't we just keep this informal. What questions do you have for me?" His notes went back in his pocket.

The room was briefly silent, but soon the first hand was raised. "Not sure there is an answer here, but how did you catch so many murderers?" Mike took a minute, "I should have been in sales." The room looked baffled. "My dad was a salesperson, he sold watches and jewellery and he was really good at it. My uncle was a salesman selling photocopiers, even my son is a salesman selling some technology for cyber security – to be honest, I have no idea what it is! I see a lot of similarities between sales and being a detective. I learnt a lot from my dad and I was really good at what I did because of the vital skills he taught me. Let me explain. Every time he had someone coming into the store he had one golden rule: find the motive. Some people would come into the store to window shop; some wanted to buy watches and jewellery for themselves; some wanted to keep up with trends; some wanted gifts for their loved ones; and so it goes on. The key to my success as a detective was always to find the motive. Find the why. It was much easier to find a killer if we knew the motive. For example, we had a case where the wife was having an affair and her partner was murdered. Once we found out about the affair we found the killer."

"So what about ones without a motive, how did you solve them?" Mike smiled. "Deep down, there is nearly always a motive, even if we don't understand it. My dad's shop was in a shopping mall and he used to say there were a hundred shops there, so why did people come into his? Sometimes there were customers who came in because they wanted to see what it was like to wear a $1,000 watch but didn't have $5 in their wallet. But the motive was there – they wanted to feel what the watch was like, to see the watch. In my experience, there is always a motive, you just have to try and find the why however deep it is hidden.

There was a young lad, probably your age, and to all appearances, he was a great person. Kind, thoughtful, worked for a charity part time, his parents were great people. One day, two teenage girls in his neighbourhood were killed. How could anyone kill them? That's where detective skills come in. You may have a suspect but no evidence, so you need to ask the right questions to find the motive. It took me a while. I didn't immediately suspect this lad, but there was something not right about him. I finally found the why – he had a crush on one of them and she rejected him. He blamed her best friend and had killed them both."

The audience was mesmerised by the detective. A few more hands quickly went up. "How has the technology police use changed over the years, and how have you adapted?" came the next question.

"Well, I'm an old man, I hate technology but, quite simply, you have to adapt to new technologies. However, I will add that I urge you to remember the basic skills you learn here and throughout your career. In my opinion, being a detective is both an art and a science." He paused, then said: "Let me share a story with you. When I started here there was no internet, DNA was not a thing and numerous other things have evolved to help us do our job. I had a mate called John who was also on the force. He was so stuck in his ways that he never really wanted to try new technology. The irony was that I eventually took on several of his old cases and I was able to solve them with the use of modern technology.

"In one case, John was convinced it was the brother of the victim who had murdered them but he couldn't prove it. I had taken the time to learn about DNA but also researched how it had helped other cops around the world. I managed to get the victim's brother's DNA after he drank a beer and that came back as a match to the crime scene. It helped to prove he was guilty. But for all the technology that was used to crack the case, it started with old-style skills. For example, you are taught to shadow and survey a suspect during your training here. That's what I did so I knew he was going to be in the bar drinking a beer that night and that was how I got the DNA. John was angry he had not solved the case and that I had done so quite simply using new methods. To this day I remind him of that. My point being, embrace the new technology; it was designed to help you but remember the core skills as well."

"Who's next?"

"I have a question for you," said a woman recruit, who just happened to be next to Charlotte. "You mentioned motive and technology and you mentioned having a suspect. But give us an example of when you don't have an initial motive or a suspect?"

"That's a great question and you will have to deal with that a lot. As I said before when you peel back the layers, there is always some sort of motive. But I'm going to share two pieces of advice here: first, who has done a jigsaw puzzle?" Lots of people raised their hands. "OK, so have any of you ever tried to do a jigsaw puzzle without seeing the picture?" Mike continued. Charlotte and a couple of others raised their hands, and Mike smiled. He used to do this game with Charlotte and her brother when they were growing up because it really tests your ability to think and be logical.

"Great. We used to call this extreme puzzling in our family. You have to look at all the pieces and start making small connections, sorting corners and straights, and sorting pieces based on patterns and colours, for example. That is how you have to approach certain cases. You need to start from the nuggets of information you have, collect every element of data. A blank notepad or whiteboard is going to be your friend. You need to jot down everything and lay out every clue or piece of information you have and then, bit by bit, start connecting the dots. Without a clear motive or technology you need to be patient.

"But there is a second piece of advice: you need to think in an unbiased way. Let me tell you an example. I had a case where a neighbour happened to be at home when the murder occurred. I spoke to him and he instantly said he saw his other neighbour at the house of the victim. That neighbour became my prime suspect – I was blinkered from there on then. That was a mistake. I needed to collect more data and have an open mind. When I did, and the blinkers were off, I discovered that the killer was actually the first neighbour I had spoken to. You need to verify things and check yourself all the time.

"Remember I said my dad was in sales? He taught me this. With a potential new client, he would do the 'detective exercise' where he mapped down everything he knew and asked a bunch of questions to clarify what he didn't know. Who they were, what was their budget, what investments had been made with other jewellery pieces, who were the key players – and the list goes on. Apparently, I became a detective by using his detective skills!" The whole room laughed.

"You need to always be asking these questions and writing down everything you have gathered. Then you ask yourself 'What more do I need? Is all the information correct? And when I mean correct, would it hold up in court as solid evidence? Am I being biased?'"

Someone raised their hand and asked, "Can you talk about that further and the importance of data?"

"Let's be clear here. The courts and judges will not convict a killer based on gut feeling. Confessions help but everyone knows people will confess even when they are innocent, and the same can be said for witnesses. People lie; data does not. But data can be manipulated. Here, let's do an experiment. Catch." Mike threw his bottle of water into the audience. One of the recruits caught it. "Throw it back," Mike said. He repeated the exercise, then said, "Imagine that was a gun used in a murder. We know from data that was the weapon that was used. We also know from fingerprint data that three of us have touched the weapon so we are all suspects. Imagine if Detective Ford was a witness. He could say I was the suspect as he saw me with the gun. But he could also say that just because he doesn't like me. With technology these days we can see who has held it the longest, how we all held it and that should be the evidence needed to reveal I'm the killer. But if you don't gather other evidence to prove this, then we are relying on one data point. So as detectives, you need to find another piece of evidence. In this example, maybe you find video evidence of me at the scene."

A young recruit, who Mike thought looked about 15, raised his hand. "These are all fantastic stories but can you tell us about a time where things didn't go to plan?"

For the first time Mike did not immediately respond, and there was an awkward silence. "I'll share a story of when things went wrong which really impacted me. Let me start by saying, you need to be vulnerable. We are all humans and we all lose, all get hurt. I haven't spoken about this story for a while, but it's an important learning point.

The best man at my wedding was a guy called Callum, who I met right here. We worked together for the first 10 years, both became detectives about the same time and spent a lot of time together out of work. He went undercover on a case and infiltrated one of the most notorious gangs in Melbourne. It went wrong and he was murdered. He was a great detective, he had a great team supporting him and there was no blame from anyone in the police force as to why it went wrong, it just did. Things are going to go wrong in this world – in life things don't always go to plan or go wrong, you have to learn to accept that. My failure here was that I lied to my family, my colleagues – everyone. I said I was OK, but I really wasn't. It got so bad I was drinking every night, my marriage was a mess and my work was suffering. I was making mistakes. I eventually got the help I needed and bounced back. But it's

OK to not be OK. You will have horrible experiences in this role. Ask for help, be vulnerable and look after yourselves." The room went silent and Mike took in a big breath.

"OK everybody, we have time for one more question for Lieutenant Gossard," said Captain Ford.

"Any final advice?" Charlotte shouted without even raising her hand.

Mike smiled. "Have an open mind, expect surprises and changes, learn to read the room or situation. For example, you're all probably thinking I'm a bad detective if you think I don't know what's going on here. I've not been asked to train new recruits for ages, so I did some research." He paused then continued. "While the team here are very good at keeping secrets and not answering my calls, I persisted and eventually found a copy of the old agenda for new recruit training – meeting an active detective isn't for another four weeks. So I concluded that something was afoot. After a bit more research I reached out to two other detectives, who I happen to know typically run these sessions." Again he paused and read the room. Then he continued.

"Detective Rowan Golden gave me great advice: be yourself, don't overthink it. I knew she was lying, though, as she would not make eye contact with me throughout. Then I spoke to Detective Scarlett Wales. She ignored my requests to meet at first but, being a detective is about persistence, especially if you have a hunch. I knew that she did a quiz at a local bar on a Tuesday night so last week I managed to 'bump' into her. I dropped into the conversation this training and she gave me very different advice to that of Detective Golden. She told me to have answers written down, to control the conversation and be prepared to include numerous cases to do actual exercises with the candidates.

"You see, when you get two people giving you different information your instincts come into play and you know someone is holding back and misleading you. I recorded both conversations and listened to them back. This is a great exercise by the way, as you often miss things while you are in the moment and much though it is uncomfortable listening to your own voice, it really has helped me get better as a Detective. My 'Aha' moment was when I listened back to Detective Wales' call. She said to be prepared for the session to last for two hours and this meeting was on my calendar for only one hour. Now I was convinced something was going to happen today. But to be sure, I drove round the car park when I arrived and saw my son's car parked at the back. Right next to it was my wife's car. They are both behind me right now, in the cove over my right shoulder. As soon as I sat down I could see people peering in and thought, 'Why would people peer in here especially when they're wearing the same shoes as my son?'"

Charlotte had heard enough. She beamed and shouted, "Surprise! You really are a good detective!" With that, the room erupted and Mike was joined by his family and a bunch of old colleagues, all there to celebrate his 35 years on the force.

The Old Coach

Eoin was enjoying his retirement. He now lived in Portugal after spending his early life in Cork, in the southern part of Ireland, then many years living in Surrey, England, a county about 20 miles from London.

Life had drastically slowed down for him now, not that he was complaining. He had earnt this. Technically, he had been working since he had turned 16, but had been in the world of football since he was a young boy, and spent over 60 years in the game. It had consumed him and it was nice to finally stop and watch the world go by. He sat on the edge of his new villa looking over the ocean and listening to the waves crash around him as the moon shone down. He had no idea how late it was but his wife, Caroline, was fast asleep. It was a Saturday night, and given that Saturday was the main day of football in the UK, he had spent much of the afternoon watching the games. He loved the game and there were bits of it he missed, especially that feeling on a Saturday night where his team had won. But being able to relax was what he needed now.

Eoin had started his football career in Ireland but as a 16-year-old had moved to London, where he had been signed to play for one of the clubs in the higher leagues. The team wasn't one of the best in London but they held their own and he was a decent player. He also represented the Republic of Ireland national team on several occasions and was very proud of that. Eoin spent 15 years at the London club, before playing for a few other smaller teams, and then retiring when he was 34.

Back in those days, he didn't earn an extortionate amount of money so, once he retired, he started a career in a bank. But he missed the game and started coaching. He quickly found out that he was a better coach than a player.

During the last 30 years, Eoin had coached numerous teams in England and Europe, including a Scandinavian national team. As a player, he had not won any trophies but, as a coach, he had an impressive record with numerous cups and a couple of league medals. Last year, he decided he needed a break. It was perfect timing as the club he was managing had been acquired by a different owner and they wanted a new manager. Now he could spend time relaxing, watching the games, walking on the beach and spending time with his family. His two daughters visited often and his four grandchildren had also come to stay several times.

He looked at his watch. It was nearly 10pm and he was tired so decided to head to bed. Just as he sipped the last of his beer, the phone rang. It was a UK number. Thinking it was a journalist, Eoin ignored it. The caller left a voicemail, explaining that it was the chairman of his first club in England. They were doing badly and they wanted him to come and manage the team for their last eight games of the season.

Fast forward to the following Tuesday morning and Eoin had landed in London and was driving to the club's training ground. He really didn't want to come out of retirement and he wasn't doing it for the money – he was doing it for the love of this club. They were in trouble and facing relegation to a lower league, which would be disastrous for the club. When a team gets relegated, it affects more than the club; it has a ripple effect throughout the community. It could mean that staff would be let go, leaving numerous families with less income; there would be less fans going to games, too, and both of these factors would impact local shops, restaurants and businesses, which would see less customers. This could lead to businesses closing and, potentially, less money being donated to local charities. The football team was the heart of this community and so relegation was not an option in Eoin's mind.

First he would review the situation, then make plans and changes. But he knew he had to act quickly. He really wanted to just get stuck in with work but first, he simply walked around the ground and the training facility before meeting the staff.

Eoin spent the rest of the week observing everything. He watched the team in training, saw who put the effort in, who listened to feedback and who was skilled. He spoke to the coaches every day, but he let them run the training sessions and pick the team for Saturday. At the game, he watched from the stands as the team got hammered 5-0. It put them bottom of the league and it was their eighth defeat in a row. Eoin had seen enough, it was time to put his plan into action.

After the game, he went into the changing room and spoke to his players for the first time. He had deliberately decided not to intervene for a week so he could simply observe but, now, it was time. "OK gents, who knows who Thomas *Edison* is?" There were a few nods around the room. "What about Abraham Lincoln, Winston Churchill or J.K Rowling? Or maybe you know David Beckham? What do they all have in common?" Eoin asked.

The room was silent before one player, Dale Jones, piped up, "They are all successful people."

"This is true," Eoin responded. "But they are also failures. Yes they all failed in life, multiple times. Because in life every failure is a learning and every failure gets you nearer to success. Remember today, remember this loss, learn from it because success will come and when it does, I want you to remember how you feel today and the journey you took to get there. I'll see you on Monday." As he left, Eoin noticed they were all clearly listening. "Good start," he thought.

On Monday morning, Eoin had the whole team line up on the training ground. Scott Webb, one of the younger players, happened to turn up late. "First things first," said Eoin. "If you are late to any meeting or training then there is a punishment. Mr Petit, you are the captain, should Mr Webb sing for us or do push ups?" Jean Petit was originally from Grenoble, in France, but had spent the last few years in England. "Sing for sure," Jean laughed. Scott Webb looked a little taken back but was a good sport and started rapping a song. Eoin had no clue what it was.

Once he was done. Eoin stepped forward. "OK, I am old enough to be most of your grandads and you may think I am out of touch with the game. That may be true, but I have won titles throughout my career as a manager and there are some fundamentals of a winning team that stand all of time. Here they are:

- Practice makes perfect
- Having a winning attitude
- Teams win titles, not players
- We have fun
- We always think next play

Over the next week, month or however long I'm in charge, we are going to focus on these five things. Make sense?"

Scott Webb chimed in, "What does *next play* mean?"

"Great question Mr Webb. Back when I was a player," Eoin started but was quickly interrupted.

"You mean during the days of horse and cart," Alex Rose, another player from the team shouted to roars of laughter.

"Funny, Mr Rose. I'm glad we're already having fun. Back when I was playing here I had a coach and he taught our team *next play*. He said we must always be thinking of *next play*: we score a goal, we celebrate then right back to positions and focus on the game again; if we concede a goal, ball out of the net, *next play*. Win a game, lose a game, concede a penalty, get sent off, score a hatrick always, always *next play*. Does that make sense to you?" The team nodded.

"Let's get to work." Eoin spent the morning running basic drills. When training was nearly done, he shouted, "Who remembers the first rule?"

"Practice makes perfect," Jean replied.

"Correct. Strikers and keepers over to one goal. I want each striker to each take five penalties to the keepers. Defenders and midfielders over to the other goal, you are going to practise running with the ball and tackling. Let's go." The players looked tired – they were normally done around this time of the day, but they got to work.

"Gents, before you leave today, we play Manchester on Saturday, they're top of the league. How many of you think we are going to win?" No one raised their hand. "Well, of course we're not going to win if you don't believe it." Eoin shouted angrily. That got the players attention, especially as he had been calm the whole morning. "I believe in every single one of you; I believe you are talented players. A million people around the country want to be in your boots, but you beat all of them to wear this shirt. You have the ability to win, but you have to believe in yourselves." With that, training was done for the day and Eoin got to work with his coaching team, analysing his players and the competition, looking at ways they could win.

He had one-on-one meetings with each of his coaching and medical staff that day. He heard the same story over and over. There was no real strategy and it made Eoin angry. The previous manager was a great player and had the brand of a celebrity; he was tipped to be one of the next best managers. But from everything Eoin had heard, he was picking players based on if he liked them or not, and more if the players loved him. He wouldn't do tactical training, just simply playing and skills and it was all about him not the club. He would spend more time on social media and signing autographs than time with his coaches.

On Tuesday, all the players turned up on time. But, Eoin dished out a punishment to two of the team as they had messy boots and were unprepared. Again they sang songs Eoin had no clue about. If nothing else he could tell his grandkids that he knew songs in the charts, he thought. Eoin had a surprise for the team as they headed to the training pitch. Normally it was just players and coaches there, but there was a small stand for spectators and today it was packed.

Eoin picked up a microphone so everyone could hear this. "Today, we have guests. Everyone in the stands works for this club – from ticket sales to the board, to security at games, those who maintain the pitch, serve you lunch or serve the fans or VIPs' lunch, our accountants, our HR team, the marketing team, our coach drivers and a few roles I have no idea what they do but am keen to learn! Before we start training today, I want you to go meet them, talk to them. A car has over a hundred different parts all of which have to work for you to be able to drive it. We are one team here and if we are to avoid relegation we all need to work, every single person at this amazing club." The players clapped and immediately ran over to 'meet' with the extended team. Eoin could see smiles and conversations.

"That was special, Coach," one of the players said as they came back. "Jack over there has been selling burgers for 30 years. I want to keep us up for him so he still has a job." Eoin smiled.

They returned to training, cheered on by the staff. At the end of the training, they did extra practice and then Eoin asked them the same question: "Who thinks we will win on Saturday?" Today, eight players raised their hands. Progress, Eoin thought.

Every day they followed the same routine, training where everyone at the club was invited and most days the stands were fairly full. It expanded quickly to include their friends and families, and local schools heard about it. Eoin was keen for the community to be involved. Every day, they did extra practice and every day he asked the whole team the same question about Saturday's game. By Friday, he had 20 hands raised.

Saturday came around and Eoin gave his players the same advice as earlier in the week. "I believe in all of you; we can win today, but remember *next play* and let's also go have fun." The game ended in a tie. No one would have bet on that result a week ago. They had equalised with a penalty that had been taken with confidence – the practice had paid off.

Monday came around and the players all turned up on time with clean boots ready for training. However, there was a note for them all on the changing room door that read: "Don't get changed, go to the second car park." The players were perplexed but did as they were told. Eoin and the coaching team were waiting for him. "Today, we're not doing training, we're going on a field trip."

"But Coach, practice makes perfect is the first rule," Jean Petit instantly said. Eoin smiled – the team was united now. "Yes, but rule three is that teams win titles not players, and rule four is we have fun. We need to embrace them today. By the way, call your families and cancel any plans as we will be together all day today."

The team boarded buses with no idea where they were going. The first stop of the day was an indoor amusement park. As they left the bus, the coaching team gave them all tickets to enter. At first, there were several escape rooms and the team was split up but the key to winning was still working as a team being a team. They played laser tag, mini golf and arcade games. Eoin was with them in the middle of it the whole time as were his coaching team – he wanted everyone involved. There was lots of laughter.

After a lunch that was totally against their usual dietary requirements, the team got back on the buses for the next stop. This was at a children's hospital where Eoin and the coaches had organised visits to sick kids. The team went around the different wards. Alex Rose was a local lad and probably one of the biggest stars on the team, and the kids' eyes lit up when they saw him. However, his face was also beaming. He insisted on delaying the next step of the day so he could get photos with every kid.

"Boss, we've decided as a team that we're going to have to come back here every month and spend more time with these kids," Jean Petit said. Then Alex Rose piped up: "Hey boys, let's ensure all those kids and parents have tickets to any game they want."

The final stop was for an early dinner. Eoin had arranged for a private room and the team played a game where they got to know everyone. Eoin found out that Alex Rose had previously been a mascot and a ballboy at the club, that his family had been season-ticket holders for three generations, and his dad ran a barbers down the road.

Jean Petit opened up about how he really struggled when he first moved to London and a team member called Charlie Hamilton revealed why he thought his form had dipped – his wife had had a miscarriage recently and he had become very distracted. "We've lost six babies, we've gone through IVF. Seeing my wife in so much pain and not being able to do anything has just consumed my mind," he said. The whole team consoled Charlie. Eoin went over to him: "Family first. You ever need time away, let me know. My wife and I lost a few kids as well, I know how tough it is."

"Thanks Boss, I really appreciate that," Charlie replied.

The day ended and the team had clearly had fun and also built camaraderie.

That weekend, the team played at home and produced their biggest win of the season with a 5-0 scoreline. Charlie Hamilton had scored a hattrick and the stadium was completely sold out.

For the next few weeks, Eoin reiterated to the team the five fundamentals:

- Practice makes perfect
- Having a winning attitude
- Teams win titles, not players

- We have fun
- We always think next play

He saw the team grow in confidence. He saw them helping each other out and he saw them smiling, which all paid off. They ended up winning the last five games and avoided relegation. Eoin had done the impossible. After the final game, he was lifted in the air, celebratory drinks were thrown over him and fans rushed to thank him. His response to everything was the same: "I've done nothing. The players and the staff here are the ones who deserve the credit."

Eoin was offered a contract to stay with the club for longer but he declined; he wanted to spend time with Caroline and his kids and grandkids at the beach.

The Babysitters

Trevor was excited but also a little nervous. Why was he getting nervous? In his 65 years on the planet, he had dealt with a lot more intimidating things. He had been a prosecuting lawyer for a top firm, had worked his way up to Partner and had handled some very notorious cases. Every time he had a big moment in court he followed a routine: have coffee with his wife, Wendy, spend 10 minutes listening to music, normally blues, then close his eyes and mediate before trying to predict what was going to happen in court or, as he called it, his battle ground. He'd then leave the house and be ready for the day. As he sat opposite Wondy drinking coffee in their backyard, he felt he needed to go through the same routine again.

It was several days after Christmas and Trevor was loving the Florida lifestyle. He checked the weather for the town in Illinois where they'd originally lived and saw that it was snowing and below zero there. Here, it was 80 degrees and not even nine in the morning.

After COVID hit in 2020, Trevor and Wendy decided it was time to move. They had two daughters but were empty nesters. Before COVID, Trevor went into the office whenever he was not travelling for work. During the isolation period, Trevor discovered that he got just as much work done at home as he did in the office. Given his firm had an office in Miami, the couple had decided to move to Aventura. It was a perfect location, nestled between two airports in case he had to travel for work, less than an hour's drive into the office and it enjoyed warm weather nearly the whole year round.

Their two daughters still lived in Illinois, one in Chicago and the other in a town in the north suburbs next to where they grew up. That was why he was nervous. His daughter, Jessie, was coming to visit with her husband Sean and their five year old daughter Liz. But Trevor's grandchild, Liz, was going to be staying with them alone as Jessie and Sean were leaving to go on their delayed honeymoon. This meant Trevor and Wendy had to entertain Liz for three days.

Trevor had raised two daughters but he wasn't as young as he used to be and it had been 30 years ago. He was excited to see his whole family but he was also a little nervous. Could he still look after children? Would Liz be OK? The timing was also far from ideal. As soon as his granddaughter left, he was due on a plane to Washington D.C. for an important case that was going to trial and he really needed to spend time working on it. But throughout his career, Trevor had always followed the rule of family first; find the balance.

When his career started and they had young kids, he often found himself in the office late or on planes and he missed softball practice or dance recitals. He hated himself for it, but he had to work. The change came when Jessie was in hospital with an infection causing her liver to fail. She went from being completely fine to being unconscious with doctors telling him she might not make it. Luckily she was put on a clinical trial and made a full recovery but that was a turning point for Trevor. He naturally dropped everything to be with his daughter and after that vowed to respect the family/work balance. Of course, there were still games he missed, but he would rather travel on a red-eye flight to ensure he got home, even if he was exhausted, than spend extra time away from his family. He tried not to travel on weekends; he blocked his calendar after 5pm so that no one could book meetings with him; and if the girls had something on or Wendy even needed a night out, he would block his calendar earlier and get an earlier train home.

Now, with his granddaughter coming to visit, he'd need to revisit his old family/work routine. He was determined to spend time with Liz, even if he was nervous about it and he would find time to get the work done, he always did. Their family arrived early in the afternoon and, after catch-ups and dinner, Jessie and Sean helped get Liz settled into bed, read her a story and snuck out. She thanked her parents and once Liz was asleep they left.

Now it was go time, Trevor thought. He stayed up late watching the child monitor closely in case she woke up but she didn't and he fell asleep. He was up early in the morning, showered and dressed before Liz was up. He was taught early in his career to be early and be prepared.

Liz eventually stirred about half an hour later and they had agreed that Wendy would go in first, get her settled and then bring her down for breakfast. That went to plan, so far so good Trevor thought. But then Trevor was reminded of how difficult it was to be a parent.

"How about waffles for breakfast?" Trevor started.

"No thanks," was Liz's response.

Trevor had anticipated he might need a second option. "Fair enough, how about cereal? Your mommy told me your favourite type."

"No thanks," Liz said a second time. Trevor was sure one of those two options would work. He changed tactics, "OK, well then what would you like?"

"Why don't you surprise me?" Liz responded with a big smile. She was having fun here, Trevor thought. He paused. He had interrogated thousands of people in the past and had got the answers he needed, he could do this with a five-year-old.

"OK, let's play a game," Trevor said. "We are going to pretend to be at a restaurant and I will give you some options for breakfast.

"Oh, that sounds like a good idea, let's go to a restaurant," Liz responded.

"Wait, that's not what I said."

"But that sounds so much fun, can we all go to a restaurant pleaaaase?"

Liz had a butter-wouldn't-melt look and Trevor caved. "OK, let's get going then," he replied.

As they were driving, Trevor wondered how it was that a five-year-old had manipulated him. He needed to negotiate better than he had; he hated losing and he had just lost to his granddaughter.

Breakfast and the morning went well, in fact, the whole day had gone well. "We've got this," Trevor thought. But he was sorely mistaken. Bedtime was a challenge. Liz had informed them she did not like the pillow, so that was changed. Then she played some different tactics to avoid going to sleep. She informed them that her parents read five books to her. Trevor knew this wasn't true but he played along; she had exhausted him and he wanted a break. But things got worse. Liz called them in the room three times for random things and then simply refused to go to bed, wanting to get into their bed instead. This went on for what seemed hours and although she eventually went to bed, Trevor felt he had clearly lost again – Liz was in charge of him.

Trevor was more prepared the next day. He went back to his negotiation training and his years in a courtroom. Once he knew who he was questioning and knew their characteristics, he had spent time prepping the questions and the tone he would use to ensure he won. He got up early and waited for Liz to come downstairs with Wendy, but this time he changed his approach.

"Good morning Liz," he said with a massive smile. He had deliberately said it with great enthusiasm. "Now, I thought long and hard about what the best breakfast could be for you and it hit me, your mom used to love my famous banana pancakes. But I'm a little rusty making them so can you help me?". Tone and body language was vital when it came to negotiation and he wanted to ensure that he had a trusting tone towards Liz.

"Sure," she responded, excited to be involved in making pancakes. "Bingo," thought Trevor. He'd got her interested in breakfast and by having her be the cook. She had even suggested a few extra ingredients.

However, the negotiation tactics continued to test Trevor throughout the day. They had decided to take Liz to a water park and she certainly tried to push barriers and negotiate everything, but she did it with such innocence.

"Can I have an ice cream, please?" she started at 9:30 in the morning.

"It's too early for ice cream now, Liz, maybe later," Trevor would reply.

"Well what time is not too early?"

"Damn," Trevor thought. He was not expecting a response. "How about after lunch?" he replied, thinking he had bought himself some time.

"Well, what time is lunch? I'm hungry now so maybe we can have lunch now, then ice cream."

Trevor needed to take back control of the conversation. "Liz, we just had breakfast and if we eat too much you will have an upset stomach when you go swimming. Let's go have fun, then eat more later."

"Is that true?" Liz turned to Wendy, but Wendy knew what was going on here and simply said "Oh yes, you can't eat too much before going swimming." Trevor winked at Wendy. Sometimes negotiation needs two, as people can feel more comfortable towards one than the other.

He often used this tactic with witnesses. He would put one of his colleagues in to question certain witnesses, especially if they had a calming demeanour. He had actually been a guest lecturer teaching students about this. Police use the same tactic all the time – the old good cop, bad cop routine.

Swimming went well and, as promised, Liz got her ice cream. The day seemed to go well, but Trevor found himself struggling to negotiate with Liz once more as bathtime came about. "I don't need a bath," she insisted. Trevor sighed. "Liz, honey, you went swimming today and played in the backyard, you are going to need a bath."

"I DON'T WANT A BATH," she screamed at the top of her lungs and slammed the door. "Of course, she would do this when Wendy had her cards evening," thought Trevor. He took a couple of deep breaths, giving Liz some time to be alone. Silence was key in negotiations; let them think he remembered being taught.

While he was studying to be a lawyer, he did cold calling during the day, selling cable TV. It was an awful job, but his manager there had taught him something that had stuck with him. "Say the pricing and then shut the hell up. The next person who spoke lost." In this case, he suspected that Liz would calm down but was probably embarrassed and wouldn't speak for a few minutes.

He calmly walked in the room and saw her under the covers of her bed. He slowly sat down at the end and let her peek round. "Hey, there she is," he said in a calming voice. "I'm sorry we had this moment. I love you dearly and I feel very bad." Start with support and caring, regain their trust. Again something he did all the time, particularly with witnesses that had had a traumatic experience. They hugged. "I understand how scary the bath must be – it's loud, it's frustrating to get in and out of it, it might not be the right temperature and you are probably really tired and don't have the energy to do a bath, am I right?" She nodded. He remembered something an old partner at a firm he worked for when he was starting his career had said. "Be empathetic, not sympathetic. Sympathy is 'I feel sorry for you,' empathy is putting yourself in their shoes. Empathy leads to trust."

"Well let me tell you why you need a bath. You see, tomorrow, we are going to go to an amusement park and then dinner, then your mom and dad will be back to pick you up. If you don't have a bath, you will likely be a bit smelly. Remember we were out in the sun all day and it was hot and I put a lot of sunscreen on you, which makes you sweat even more. Now I don't care if you smell, but the amusement park people might not let you in."

"Can they do that?" asked Liz.

"I know this the hard way. See, I went fishing last year. I caught a lot of fish and then went to the park, but they said I smelled of fish too bad and didn't let me in." This wasn't exactly true. He had gone fishing last year and Wendy had flat out told him he needed to shower before going anywhere in the house, and also told him they had dinner plans and she wasn't going with someone that smelt like a trout! However, Trevor had remembered that telling stories resonates with people.

"OK, I will take a bath," said Liz and walked off to the bathroom. Trevor sighed with deep relief; that took a lot out of him.

Trevor and Wendy both woke up early the next morning and were prepared for the day. Trevor was a lot closer to Liz after the last few days, something he would cherish. He also thought he could now anticipate her moods and how she communicated with him. That would help their relationship.

There was another twist when she woke up this time."Grandad, can I have a chocolate croissant for breakfast?

I saw you had the mix in the fridge," asked Liz. "Nothing gets past her," Trevor thought.

"Well let me teach you something. Do you know what I did as a job?" Trevor asked.

"You're a grandad, you spend time here and you drink lots of coffee and read lots of books," came the reply.

Trevor laughed. "This is true but I am also a lawyer and my job is to put bad people in jail. The police would catch them and I would do something called 'present and negotiate' to ensure the bad people went to jail."

"Cooooool," Liz said, and Trevor was surprised how interested she was. His own children had never wanted to talk about his career. He continued, "Negotiating means two people coming together to make an agreement."

"Like you and me coming to an agreement over ice cream yesterday."

"Exactly," Trevor said with excitement. "Someone told me that negotiation is all about give and take, so in this case, if I make you chocolate croissants what will you give me?"

Liz paused for a moment then said, "I like this game. I will make my bed and get ready now if you make me chocolate croissants." Trevor smiled. He wished he'd had this conversation with Liz on day one but still he'd made progress. "Deal," he said and put her hand out to shake it.

This experiment went on for the whole day.

"Grandad, can we go on the carousel first? If you let me do this, I will promise to go on the big wheel as I remembered you said you liked it."

"Liz, can you please go use the restroom with your grandma? If you do, then we can have a donut after."

"Make it a funnel cake grandad!"

Both of them were clearly having fun with this new game. Wendy was laughing to herself the whole time. She could see how happy Trevor was with Liz. They left the amusement park and Trevor thought his time negotiating with his granddaughter was over, but there was one more twist and Trevor had played this one with his own children.

"Grandad, can we have a burger for dinner?"

"Grandad, how about a burger for dinner?"

"Grandad, you know what is yummy? Burgers, we should have that for dinner."

"Grandad, Grandma and I were talking about dinner, you know what we want? Burger."

"Burger, burger, burger!"

Trevor finally caved. "Hey, Liz, how about we make burgers for dinner from the grill when your parents arrive?"

"That sounds like a great idea," she replied seriously. Trevor didn't have the energy to fight her and he had done the same in court, reiterating the same question but presenting it in different ways for years.

That evening, with Jessie and Sean back, they were having dinner together, when Liz said: "Mommy, I love Grandma and Grandad. I had such fun and Grandad taught me to negotiate!"

www.ingramcontent.com/pod-product-compliance
Lightning Source LLC
Chambersburg PA
CBHW050311230526
45471CB00005B/2133